LGBTQ Catholics

LGBTQ Catholics

A GUIDE TO INCLUSIVE MINISTRY

Yunuen Trujillo

Paulist Press
New York / Mahwah, NJ

Cover image by Zaie/Shutterstock.com
Cover and book design by Lynn Else

"Parents' Prayer" in Appendix C composed by parent members of the Archdioceses of Los Angeles, Catholic Ministry with Lesbian and Gay Persons © 1996. Used with permission.
"You Know My Voice" composed by Lynette Aldapa of *Comunidad*, the gay and lesbian ministry of St. Matthew Parish, Long Beach, of the Los Angeles Archdiocese Catholic Ministry with Lesbian and Gay Persons © 1996. Used with permission.

Library of Congress Cataloging-in-Publication Data
Names: Trujillo, Yunuen, author.
Title: LGBTQ Catholics : a guide to inclusive ministry / Yunuen Trujillo.
Description: New York / Mahwah : Paulist Press, [2022] | Includes bibliographical references. | Summary: "LGBTQ Catholics presents a guide that encompasses the different levels of ministry and that gives a full-picture template to serve as a model that can be replicated in any parish communities around the world"—Provided by publisher.
Identifiers: LCCN 2021042811 (print) | LCCN 2021042812 (ebook) | ISBN 9780809155774 (paperback) | ISBN 9781587689765 (ebook)
Subjects: LCSH: Church work with gays—Catholic Church. | Church and minorities. | Sexual minorities—Religious life.
Classification: LCC BX1795.H66 T78 2022 (print) | LCC BX1795.H66 (ebook) | DDC 261.8/35766—dc23
LC record available at https://lccn.loc.gov/2021042811
LC ebook record available at https://lccn.loc.gov/2021042812

ISBN 978-0-8091-5577-4 (paperback)
ISBN 978-1-58768-976-5 (e-book)

Published by Paulist Press
997 Macarthur Boulevard
Mahwah, New Jersey 07430
www.paulistpress.com

Printed and bound in Colombia

God loves you, and he loves you unconditionally.
To all those LGBTQ Catholics who have not
been told this often enough,
and to those who are hearing it for the first time.

CONTENTS

FOREWORD

For more than fifty years, I have been a pastoral minister for LGBTQ Catholics. In 1971, when I became friends with gay Catholics at the University of Pennsylvania while I was doing my graduate work, I heard countless LGBTQ Catholics ask, "Why should I stay in this Church that doesn't want me?" "Should I join the Episcopal Church?" or "Should I dissociate myself from all organized religion and become a 'none,' a spiritual person but not religious?"

Because God's grace caused me to stumble into lesbian-gay ministry, as it was called fifty years ago, I too faced difficult situations with the institutional church so that many people asked me, "Why do you stay in the Catholic Church?" For me, a cradle Catholic, educated for eighteen years in Catholic institutions, a member of a religious congregation of women for more than sixty years, a person with a historical view of religion and the forces of change, there has never been any hesitation. The advocate and reformer in me want to help make the Catholic Church, which I love, a beloved community that follows the gospel and walks in the footsteps of Jesus. The Catholic Church is my spiritual home.

I have often had, and still have, disagreements with family members; sometimes our points of view are diametrically opposite. But I could never renounce my family. They are my hereditary and first home; for good and ill, they helped shape me into the person I am today. These two homes—family and Catholic Church—are part of my mystical fiber.

This question, "Why stay in the Catholic Church?" continues to be asked today by LGBTQ Catholics and is repeated in this fine book. At one point in her compelling story, Yunuen Trujillo asks herself this same question, "Why stay?" Yes, much is the same.

But much has changed. The website of New Ways Ministry lists hundreds of LGBTQ friendly parishes across the United States, but most do not have formal outreach ministries. These parishes, and thousands of others, need this book!

LGBTQ Catholics: A Guide to Inclusive Ministry will help parishes begin such a ministry. This book is a Catholic primer with all the right tools. It offers definitions, information to dispel myths and stereotypes, models of ministry, basic Church teaching, and so much more. I was struck by Yunuen Trujillo's spirituality and how often she returns again and again to the fundamentals of the Catholic faith found in the Gospels: respect, compassion, and love for all human beings because we have been created in the image and likeness of God.

Yes, our Catholic parishes need ministries for LGBTQ people and their families, not only for those who feel marginalized, but also for the parishioners themselves who are called to live out the social doctrine of the Church. To be truly Catholic, our Church needs to embrace and welcome *all* God's people.

And, of course, LGBTQ parish ministry is much needed so that LGBTQ Catholics, who have felt like outsiders, may feel the love and warmth of being an insider in their own Church. Only then will we create a spiritual home so that LGBTQ Catholics will no longer ask themselves, "Why stay?"

Jeannine Gramick, SL

INTRODUCTION

The concept of inclusive LGBTQ ministry is not new. For decades, a handful of ministries in the United States and other countries have been working hard to create welcoming spaces for LGBTQ Catholics. Some of them have done it while being in good standing with the Church; others have been inspired to push the boundaries more. Regardless, all these ministries have provided a safe place, an oasis in the desert for LGBTQ Catholics. Their presence has been prophetic and the result of divine inspiration, the inspiration that God gives each of those called to serve, and to serve in the margins.

Historically, some of these ministries have been more public than others about their pastoral mission, but the truth is that most of them are not known to the general Catholic population. Much of the work they have done has remained unpublished and hidden. Some of the wisdom in ministry they have accumulated over the years has been written down, but there are not many materials that provide a comprehensive overview of LGBTQ ministry.

Over the last few years, in making positive statements about LGBTQ Catholics, Pope Francis has achieved something very simple. He has broken the silence on a topic that was often considered taboo and started a dialogue and a process of discernment, which has raised the question for the Church: How can we better serve, welcome, and offer inclusive pastoral care to LGBTQ Catholics and their families?

LGBTQ Catholics are no longer invisible. While the Catholic Church—both the institution and the people—still have a long way to go in this process of discernment, dialogue on this topic has started and will continue. The Holy Spirit, the *Ruah*, is moving. She is inspiring dialogue, and she has inspired this book.

I have had the privilege of presenting workshops on this topic at parishes, regional congresses, and even at the Los Angeles Religious Education Congress, the largest Catholic congress in the world. At the end of the workshops there is always someone who says, "Okay, this sounds great! But how can I now take this to my parish, my diocese, my country, when there are no books with this content, only the workshops given here?" This book is an answer to that question, to that plea.

Not all the answers to the difficult questions on this topic can be found here. (God knows, there is still a lot that we as humans must unravel humbly in the knowledge of the Divine and of creation). If anything, this book will generate more questions, as it is meant to be a dialogue starter; it is a beginning, not an end. This book begins a process of discernment. Like any discernment process, both personal and institutional, it might take years, but it must start now.

For years, LGBTQ Catholics have had to hide in fear and anguish for fear of losing what is most sacred to them: Catholic community and a space to further one's relationship with God. Often to avoid creating discomfort, LGBTQ Catholics have had to be invisible and have suffered violence and discrimination in the process. We are a vulnerable group and vulnerable groups must be at the center of the gospel.

This book would not have been possible if it weren't for the wisdom and kindness of those who have shared their knowledge in ministry selflessly for many years. I particularly raise the names of Fr. Chris Ponnet and Dr. Arthur Fitzmaurice, who compiled over the years some of the documents referred to here. There are many others who have been instrumental in the creation of this book, amazing women and men, who have opened doors for me along the way. Some of them and their stories are mentioned in this book. Finally, this would not have been possible without the care of my spiritual directors, and the unconditional love of friends and family.

Hopefully, this book will be one of many more to address inclusive LGBTQ ministry.

I

THE NEED FOR
A MINISTRY

WHEN A CHILD "COMES OUT"

Martha Plascencia and Jenny Naughton met in 1991 while taking their respective children to Boy Scouts meetings and have become close friends. Both were confirmation teachers at their parish in Diamond Bar, California, and over the years, have been involved in several other ministries. In 2005, their respective worlds changed when their sons came out of the closet.

Martha's and Jenny's responses were very accepting; they loved their sons, and nothing was going to change that. Yet, at the same time, they had many questions about what the future would look like for their sons. They each realized that a significant journey was ahead of them and that they needed to accompany each other on their journey. As mothers of LGBTQ children, they now had to go through a faith journey that was different from that of other Catholic parents. Although their parish had a variety of ministries, there was none that effectively catered to the specific needs of parents with LGBTQ children, as the topic itself was taboo. Their parish community, as is often the case in many parishes today, was ill-equipped to accompany them on their journey. They realized the need for a ministry that was not being met.

1

It is said that when a child, a son or daughter of any age, "comes out of the closet," the parent goes into the closet. While the person coming out has had time to discern the difficult questions that come with assuming and affirming one's orientation or identity, the parents have often never pondered those questions. For the parents, the day their child "comes out" might be the first time they even think about those difficult questions; they are often unable or unwilling to talk about the topic, are in denial, or express a variety of other isolating attitudes. Often, this type of reaction doesn't mean that the parents don't love their child but rather they are starting on a long process of discernment and don't know where to go.

The most common concern for parents is the well-being and physical safety of the child, followed by a concern for the salvation of the child's soul; these concerns are closely followed by other concerns regarding the safety and well-being of the parents themselves—and thoughts of guilt, fear, and trying to pinpoint *why* their child is gay. Parents often ask questions such as the following: "Will my child be all right physically?" "Will my child have work and financial stability?" "What will my extended family say about my child?" "What will our friends from church say about my child?" "Does this mean I have to choose between my child and the Church?" "Will I now be excluded from any church ministries?" "What will people say about me and my ability to parent?" "What did I do wrong?" "Why is God punishing me?" "Why is my child gay?" "Why didn't he tell me this before?" "Will I go to heaven if my child is gay?"

These questions often express themselves in the form of fear, anger, denial, and sadness, among other expressions. At times, the fear, anger, denial, or sadness are not expressed at all, and are conveyed through silence—a long, hard, painful silence. Regardless, these feelings can tear families apart.

To be fair, not all parents are surprised when their child

comes out. Many parents have known or suspected that their child is *different* and have faced their fears ahead of time. By the time their child comes out, those parents have already taken the time to think about the difficult questions and have gone through the discernment process ahead of the event. In the best situations, the parents' response is positive and affirming of God's love: "I will always love you. You will always be my child."

Many catechists and lay ministers are experiencing situations like this more often than they are willing to admit. They are asking themselves these same questions after a loved one—their child, their grandchild, sibling, or family friend—comes out of the closet, and they are going through these processes in silence and alone, feeling torn between their love for their child and their Church. These people, part of the Body of Christ, our Church, are hurting and have nowhere to turn, no community within the Church where they can be open about their journey without being criticized or judged. Often, the first instinct is to talk to a priest in confession, but parents of LGBTQ Catholics have no community where they can unconditionally walk with each other in their journey of faith and discernment.

THE LGBTQ PERSON

Of course, we must not forget the other part of the Body of Christ, our Church, that is hurting: the LGBTQ person. Shortly after I came out to my pastor in 2015, he introduced me to Irma and another LGBTQ parishioner, so that the three of us could find community in each other. He jokingly called us the Holy Trinity, a nickname that we certainly embraced.

Irma had been a Catholic school student from kindergarten through high school. To use her own words, she was "the perfect mold" of a good Catholic education, but she was much more than that. She truly was, and is, a Catholic at heart—a kind, loving, and giving soul. Shortly after she came out, however, things changed. The community who saw her grow up, the community that she had relied on and had believed would always be there for her, struggled to reconcile their love for her with what they believed was the "right" response, the response that the Church required of them. Some of her closest friends deserted her and insisted that they had to tell her the "truth." Others simply distanced themselves. Her best friend stopped talking to her and many others judged her. She had known she was different since the age of five, and she was still the same person—a kind, loving, and giving soul—she had been before she came out, yet something had painfully changed. Her parents, who loved her deeply, also struggled reconciling the dreams they had envisioned for her with the new reality.

Irma ended up attending a good Catholic university far away from home and is now a college graduate. She is still Catholic, but she knows that nothing she can do can put her back on that pedestal people had placed her when she was in high school, even though she is still the same person, and perhaps now even a better person. She knows her family loves her. Her hope is that one day her actions will speak for themselves. She believes that being a true Christian should not pull her away from living a happy, kind, fulfilling, and loving life, and that people will recognize the good in her. She also realizes how much pain everything that happened has caused her and that she is still healing from the pain caused by the Church, the people of God. Nevertheless, she is hopeful that one day those who love her and those who deserted her will accept her as she is.

For much of my life, I have been a lay minister in Catholic young adult ministry, and a lay minister in Catholic LGBTQ Ministry for more than seven years. As a lay minister, I have heard hundreds of heartbreaking stories involving LGBTQ persons. These heartbreaking stories include stories of family and community rejection, violence, bullying, suicide attempts, depression, abuse and discrimination in the workplace, homelessness, and poverty. But there is nothing more heartbreaking than realizing that many of these painful stories start with a history of rejection by a church minister (lay or ordained), a family member heavily involved in the Church, or any other person who claims to speak on behalf of God. These stories damage what is most pure in the human being: the soul and the desire for closeness with God.

Desmond Tutu once said, "A person is a person through other persons; you can't be human in isolation; you are human only in relationships." When the LGBTQ person is rejected, marginalized, and excluded from the most sacred community a human being can have—family—it is devastating and dehumanizing. But when the rejection is by the church community or by someone claiming to speak on God's behalf, not only does it hurt our deepest human fibers; it also robs us of our very own dignity as children of God. It is the worst kind of violence because it wounds the soul.

Consequently, many LGBTQ persons leave the Church because it is too painful to be invisible, to be treated as if we were less than a full person, and not feel part of the community. But there are also many of us who stay. We are all a part of the Body of Christ.

THE LGBTQ CATHOLIC

I am an LGBTQ Catholic. Many people have asked in the past why I choose to refer to myself as an "LGBTQ Catholic" as opposed to a "homosexual," a person with "*same-sex attraction*," or some other term the Church generally uses. I choose to refer to myself as an LGBTQ Catholic because this term acknowledges my full humanity, focusing on the fact that I am first and foremost a person, a child of God who adheres to the Catholic faith, a person with a spiritual life and longing.

DID YOU KNOW?

"LGBT" stands for Lesbian, Gay, Bisexual, and Transgender, and is part of the longer anachronym: LGBTQIA+. The "Q" stands for Questioning (someone who is still in their discernment process), or "Queer," which is another umbrella term for someone who is not heterosexual but does not want to be judged by preconceived ideas or prejudice. The "I" stands for Intersex (a small group of people born with a quantifiable variation in their chromosomes that results in ambiguous genitalia or other physical characteristics that usually define "male" or "female"), and the "A" stands for Asexual (people who do not have any sexual feelings or sexual attraction toward others). It is very important for Catholic communities to understand these terms to avoid treating someone with prejudice out of not knowing what these terms mean. For purposes of this book, the term *LGBTQ*, includes everyone listed above: LGBTQIA+.

At the same time, the term *LGBTQ Catholic* states that I am marginalized because of either my sexual orientation or my identity. People who are unfamiliar with the term *LGBTQ* often feel uncomfortable using such a general term because they need to know exactly "what I am," because people often have a need to label the *other* to differentiate themselves. However, labels often come with prejudice and preconceived ideas that do not represent who we really are. It is my hope that this book will help people see the person before them, the Catholic, without the need of a label, and set their prejudices aside so that we can see the real person.

AVOIDING STEREOTYPES

LGBTQ Catholics have always been, are, and will continue to be present in the Church throughout all levels of ecclesial life. We are not an "outside force" that threatens to defile the purity of the Church; rather, we are part of the Church. There are many stereotypes about LGBTQ Catholics, but it is only through encountering one that you can learn something of who the person really is.

First, there is the myth, for example, that LGBTQ people are not interested in religion, church community, or even God—that *"there is no such thing as a gay Catholic."* In fact, LGBTQ persons, just like everyone else, have a deep desire to be connected with the source of life, whom we most often identify as love or simply God. God, the source of all love, is constantly calling us to live a more genuine and fruitful life. We desire to find community in the Church—a space where we can continue relating to God regardless of how we discern our spiritual journey. Some of us find community and stay in the Church, but often, such space is nonexistent. The Church can often be an emotionally unhealthy space for LGBTQ Catholics. Because many needs are not being met, many LGBTQ Catholics leave the Church. Some find spiritual spaces in other religious traditions or philosophical practices; others are just so hurt by the rejection of someone who represented religion or God in their life that they prefer to walk away from anything that resembles religion. Yet, God continues calling us wherever we go.

Those who stay, however, are everywhere: we are parishioners who sit on the pews every Sunday; we are choir members who lead you in songs of worship; we are catechists who help others learn the foundations of the faith; we are ministers in prayer groups and eucharistic ministers; we are children in your religious education programs and youth in your Catholic schools; we are staff members; we are also priests and religious sisters and brothers at all levels of ecclesial life. You have certainly met one or more LGBTQ Catholic during your ministry. We may be people whom you care about deeply and possibly even admire for our faith. Many LGBTQ Catholics choose not to share this information, at least not yet, because we don't feel we are in a safe place or because we are still in a process of discernment or denial. Maybe some of us are yet to discover the truth about ourselves. However, just because we don't look or act the way you think we are supposed to look or act, doesn't mean we don't exist.

Second, each of us may choose different terminology to identify ourselves, but just because we use a specific term doesn't mean we can be stereotyped. For example, just because some of us choose to identify as gay, lesbian, bisexual, or transgender does not mean that we are promiscuous or even sexually active at any given moment. Furthermore, just because some of us may identify as "persons with same-sex attraction," does not mean that we are repressed or brainwashed nor that we are better or worse than someone else. Each of us has a different understanding or level of comfort with a specific word or terminology and each has a different journey that cannot be stereotyped. We are all going through a process of self-discernment on our spiritual journey.

In my ministry, I have learned to acknowledge and respect the other's journey whenever possible and to avoid stereotypes. I have met LGBTQ Catholics who are still questioning (or discerning) their sexual orientation and identity and how public they want these to be. I have also met some LGBTQ Catholics who are discerning a religious vocation, others who are single and feel called to abstain from having sex, and others who feel called to finding a lifelong partner. I have met LGBTQ Catholics who are searching for their soul mate through dating and others who already have a partner to whom they are faithful. I have met ordained LGBTQ Catholics who have taken a vow of celibacy that they honor and cherish. I have met some LGBTQ Catholics who are asexual and are simply not interested in sexual relationships, and others who are not asexual but are interested in having a partner for the company and emotional rather than sexual connection. Finally, I have met some LGBTQ Catholics whose relationship goals and self-understanding have changed over time.

In other words, everyone is different, and each of us has our own lived experience and story to tell. The LGBTQ person is far more than simply a sexual orientation or identity. We possess a spiritual longing, with life goals and dreams, with virtues and shortcomings, with God-given gifts and talents, with a capacity for self-knowledge and self-determination, with interests and needs beyond sexual orientation and identity, and with favorite foods and artists; we are as complex, varied, loved, and holy as any other human being made in the image of God, *imago Dei*, and born into a community with a dignity that must be respected. Some LGBTQ Catholics have endured unimaginable pain, and all the challenges that come with it, but they strive to be the best they can with what they have on their own spiritual journeys, sometimes alone and other times with community. For these reasons, there is no place for stereotypes.

LGBTQ CATHOLIC CLERGY

For those ordained LGBTQ Catholics, who made a promise to remain celibate, and for those religious sisters and brothers at various levels of ecclesial life, it is often even harder to speak publicly or offer self-reflection on this topic, because there is a fear that they will be misunderstood or misjudged. A couple years ago, I met a priest who was visiting from abroad. We were both speakers at the yearly Los Angeles Religious Education Congress and were chatting in the speaker's lounge. While I was explaining to him the ministry I do, he commented, "It is really good that a layperson is talking about this topic. We need laypeople because it is harder for us priests to talk about it."

I have met some very holy and dedicated celibate priests who are LGBTQ Catholics. Of course, they do not tell anyone that they are LGBTQ, and why should it matter? It is often better left unsaid. In addition to responding to a call to chastity like all people—heterosexual and homosexual persons—priests also vow a life of celibacy. So, why should it matter? Yet these holy and dedicated priests are often afraid of sharing their story because of people's misconceptions and prejudice.

PEDOPHILIA

A common misconception is the identification of being gay with being a pedophile. The sexual abuse of children is a crime that must be eliminated in all circles where it presents itself; particularly in the Church, which is a place where vulnerable persons should be even more protected. The past failures of the Church to address cases of child sexual abuse properly has created a ripple effect that is contrary to the gospel and will continue driving people away from the Church until it is fully addressed. However, it must be noted that pedophilia is present in adults of all races and sexual orientations.

Over the past few years, I have taught a class in Spanish on Catholic social teaching as part of a formation program for young adults ("Pastoral Juvenil") in the Archdiocese of Los Angeles. In recent years, I have included the issue of child abuse as part of the curriculum where I include the following activity with very similar results. First, I ask the attendants to close their eyes. Second, I ask people to raise their hand, with eyes closed, if they know of someone in their extended family who was touched inappropriately as a child and/or abused by another family member. Almost every time, several hands in the group go up, usually close to 50 percent. With their eyes still closed, I ask people to keep their hand up if the abuser in that situation was a heterosexual family member. Most people keep their hand raised.

While the findings in this activity are more empirical than scientific, two things always catch my attention. First, the issue of pedophilia is not only more common than most people think, but it is prevalent in many extended families. However, it seems as if it is mostly women who are either aware of it or willing to acknowledge or talk about it, for most of the people who raise their hand during this exercise tend to be women. Perhaps their own mothers warned them about a specific family member who was a molester or maybe they just found out on their own. This does not mean that men are not also victims; men just seem to be less willing to talk about it, which makes other men not aware. Second, pedophiles come in all sexual orientations as do the victims of pedophilia. Any bishop or priest who is close enough to their community, the Body of Christ, to hear the painful stories of abuse by family members in confession, will know that child abuse is a persistent problem occurring in families and that pedophiles are people from all sexual orientations.

Within the Church, child sexual abuse has its own characteristics that are different from those of a family, yet the basic elements of pedophilia are still the same. While pedophile priests and supporters of clericalism continue to scapegoat gay priests, the issue of clerical child sexual abuse will never be solved. Note that Catholic theology regarding homosexuality does not see a homosexual orientation as sinful. Despite this, gay priests in the Catholic Church who are celibate and chaste continue to fear judgment and are often unable to defend themselves, because our Church leaders have not spoken often enough about the God-given gifts of gay and lesbian persons or about our innate dignity as children of God. Furthermore, our Church leaders often fail to differentiate between a gay sexual orientation and pedophilia, often conflating both.

Hopefully, we can overcome this myth. We must stop conflating an LGBTQ orientation or identity with pedophilia if we are to be true to our Catholic mission.[1] Pedophilia has no place in the Church regardless of race, orientation, identity, rank, or any other differentiating characteristic.

---

1.   For an analysis and recommendations by fifty prominent lay Catholic leaders regarding the sexual abuse crisis, see Initiative on Catholic Social Thought and Public Life, "Report of the National Convening on Lay Leadership for a Wounded Church and Divided Nation," Georgetown University, November 4, 2019, https://catholic socialthought.georgetown.edu/publications/report-of-the-national-convening-on-lay -leadership-for-a-wounded-church-and-divided-nation. For an analysis of sexual abuse in the Church, see Yunuen Trujillo, "Clerical Sexual Abuse: Religious Institutions Must Have a Pentecost Moment and They Must Have It Now," Berkley Forum, Georgetown University, September 25, 2019, https://berkleycenter.georgetown.edu/responses/ clerical-sexual-abuse-religious-institutions-must-have-a-pentecost-moment-and-they -must-have-it-now.

3

CREATING INCLUSIVE LGBTQ MINISTRIES

Whenever I give a workshop about LGBTQ ministry at Religious Education Congresses, I hear heartbreaking stories. Catechists and ministers who have been involved in the Church for many years come to me for guidance and community because someone they know has come out. I often suggest they read "Always Our Children," a pastoral letter written by the United States Conference of Catholic Bishops in 1997.[1] It states, "This child, who has always been God's gift to you, may now be the cause of another gift: your family becoming more honest, respectful, and supportive." Your child will always be your child. Nothing can ever change that. Your child is also a child of God.

While this pastoral letter is helpful for parents, parents of LGBTQ children often need a space where they can be accompanied in their journey and where they can accompany each other, unconditionally. Recalling Martha's and Jenny's experiences from the first chapter, after their children came out, they had nowhere to turn for guidance and community. When they saw the need for ministry, they decided to create a support group for parents of LGBTQ Catholics in their parish. This ministry, Always Our Children, named after the pastoral letter, has

---

1. National Conference of Catholic Bishops, *Pastoral Letters of the United States Catholic Bishops*, vol. 6, ed. Patrick W. Carey (Washington, DC: United States Catholic Conference, 1998), 840–50.

evolved since it first began and has given rise to what is now called No Barriers to Christ.

LGBTQ Catholics have also started to create safe spaces for themselves in parish communities. Cynthia is a fellow parishioner and LGBTQ Catholic and, along with Irma and me, is the third person of our "holy trinity." Cynthia is an exemplary Catholic, who was discerning religious life until a religious sister mistakenly told her that she could not be a religious if she is gay. This was heartbreaking news for her. She stopped discerning religious life and decided to start a parish ministry for LGBTQ Catholics called Agape. However, she had difficulty finding resources for guidance as to how to start such a ministry. Despite the lack of resources, she created a wonderful, vibrant, and well-organized ministry. While her work was truly admirable and was fully supported by our pastor, certain people in the community opposed it and some of Cynthia's friends distanced themselves from her. Since then, Cynthia has parted ways with the Church, but the ministry survived and has become her legacy. It has brought healing and has created a space for others.

Generally, LGBTQ ministries can be characterized as either ministries by and for parents of LGBTQ Catholics— such as Martha and Jenny's ministry Always Our Children—or as ministries by and for LGBTQ persons—such as Cynthia's Agape. In practice, however, parents and LGBTQ persons are welcome at both. When I came out in 2014, I started attending Martha and Jenny's parent ministry meetings. Even though most of the people were parents of LGBTQ Catholics and the group was intended for parents, they welcomed me, patiently listened to me, and allowed me to cry with them. By listening to their experiences as parents I was able to understand my own family and their journey better. By listening to my experience as an LGBTQ Catholic, I hope they were also better able to understand their children. These parents asked me to stay in the Church and to serve and minister with them. In fact, I would not have stayed had it not been for them. Therefore, while we can categorize our ministries as either ministries for parents of LGBTQ Catholics or as ministries for LGBTQ persons, everyone is welcome at both.

There are many challenges in creating a ministry for parents of LGBTQ Catholics and/or a ministry for LGBTQ persons. The first challenge is the fact that there are very few centralized resources to offer basic guidance for LGBTQ ministry, including, for example, the kinds of ministries that can be created, how to create them, their purpose and mission, the most common challenges, and how to overcome them, among other things.

In responding to these questions, this chapter will focus primarily on parish ministries and five other important categories of ministry: diocesan/archdiocesan, religious orders, Catholic higher education, national ministries, and international ministries. While not an exhaustive study of all these categories or the challenges that these ministries face, this chapter will present a variety of experiences, best practices, and advice. Many of the examples are from ministries based in the United States, but some are from ministries from overseas where the same general categories can be found.

PARISH MINISTRY

Purpose and Mission

Parish ministry is a grassroots ministry in that it has the most direct contact with the people of God and their daily life. Parish ministry is often the first contact for someone in distress, and the one that focuses on serving LGBTQ Catholics and their parents.

Pastoral Care

The purpose and mission of our ministries should always be centered on pastoral care. Pastoral care is like being companions on a journey. Fr. Raniero Alessandrini, CS, notes, "Through the centuries, community leaders have given care, support, and guidance during personal crises and losses." The coming-out process is full of personal crises and losses because it often triggers a crisis in the family. This crisis affects both the parents and the LGBTQ child. For those who have worked in LGBTQ ministry, we know that the amount of pain and anguish and the potential for family separation through this crisis is high. Consequently, the primary purpose of any LGBTQ ministry is to attend to that pain and to accompany this part of the Body of Christ through their journey and process.

Just as the wounds in a medical emergency are assessed and triaged with the most urgent ones being attended to first, effective pastoral care during this stage should be focused on the pain being experienced by *listening to the person* who comes to the ministry and refraining from attempts to teach Church doctrine, unless a specific inquiry has been made by the person seeking assistance and support.

Following this initial stage, LGBTQ Catholics and their parents must still go through a lifelong and continuing process of discernment that includes learning how to relate to God and to one another based on this new reality. Therefore, offering a *safe space* for discernment is another important role of pastoral care. All of us—gay and straight—must constantly discern a multitude of questions about ourselves, our lives, God, our vocations, our careers, our fears, and our goals and dreams. However, the LGBTQ person is often excluded from such discernment in the Church, often being told what to do, what "vocation" is possible, and being reduced to only one aspect of their being.

As an LGBTQ person, I can attest that this personal process of discernment is extremely important. Without such discernment, it is easy to base the foundations of one's life on fears rather than on one's calling. Thanks to my own process of discernment, I have a solid foundation and a deep faith and love for Jesus, which has helped me to continue in his Church despite all the hurt I have experienced. Creating safe spaces for discernment is an important role of pastoral care.

Often the best companions on our journeys of faith are people who have already gone through the journey themselves—LGBTQ Catholics accompanying other LGBTQ Catholics and their parents accompanying other parents. However, we encourage all lay and ordained ministers to learn more about the journeys of LGBTQ Catholics and that of their parents.

Inclusiveness

Because our ministries are inclusive, the pastoral care we offer is not conditioned on the status of any specific relationship. All people are welcome in our ministries and their processes of discernment are encouraged and respected regardless of the result. Our purpose is not to indoctrinate, but to accompany, guide, and offer a safe space for discernment alongside Jesus. While discussions about Church doctrine and faith formation are commonplace in our ministries, they emerge from a place of respect for the lived experience of the LGBTQ person and with an openness to the message of the Holy Spirit and the signs of the times.

For ministers to offer effective pastoral care to marginalized populations, therefore, three aspects of Church are extremely helpful: listening, encounter, and accompaniment. While these three aspects will be analyzed more in depth in chapter 5, let us summarize, here, how they apply to LGBTQ ministry:

A Listening Church. LGBTQ ministry provides safe spaces where we all *listen* to and learn from each other's lived experience without judgment. Through listening, we *learn*, as opposed to listening to "respond" or to "fix" or to "give advice." We also try to guide each other through the journey based on our own lived experience and, most of all, based in Jesus and the gospel of love. We find our strength in prayer and community and rely on pastoral documents, such as the pastoral letter "Always our Children." We also invite and encourage our pastors to join our meetings.

A Church of Encounter. LGBTQ ministry provides safe spaces where we can *encounter* each other where we are in our journey, not where others think we should be. This is important because people who come to our ministry come from different walks of life and lived experiences, so we must encounter each other as we are. All are welcome, unconditionally.

A Church of Accompaniment. LGBTQ ministry provides safe spaces where we can *accompany* each other through our very different, yet similar, journeys of faith, no matter what that journey looks like. In other words, the pastoral care needs to be inclusive and affirming.[2]

Finally, an unnamed but implicit purpose of LGBTQ ministry is always spiritual growth and a deepening of the faith through our lived experiences. The amount of time and resources dedicated to different techniques of spiritual growth depends on the model of ministry each ministry follows.

MODELS OF PARISH MINISTRY

There are two models of parish ministry: the support group model and the evangelization model. In my experience,

---

2. For sample mission/vision statements of existing LGBTQ ministries, see appendix B.

most parent ministries follow a *support group model*, while LGBTQ ministries usually follow either the *support group model* or an *evangelization model*. Each model comes with its own challenges and advantages that ministry leaders are encouraged to analyze before deciding which one to follow.

Support Group Model

The support group model is the simplest and sometimes the most effective for offering pastoral care.

Characteristics

Support groups usually meet once a month either on church property or in a private location. When Martha and Jenny began their ministry for parents, they published it in the parish bulletin: *"We hope to see you at 7 p.m. in Hall B."* At that first meeting, no one showed up. They wondered why and decided to try meeting in one of their homes instead. The next month, the parish bulletin announced: *"We hope to see you on this day at 7 p.m., call X phone number for more info."* At that second meeting, folks from their parish showed up. When asked why they had not shown up the previous month, people said they felt afraid that others in the parish community would see them going to a gay ministry meeting and would know that a loved one is gay. While support groups can meet either on parish grounds or in private locations, support groups that meet at private locations tend to be more successful for this reason.

Regardless of location, the support group format is simple. Everyone sits in a circle facing each other, and the group usually starts with a prayer or a short reflection on the gospel. Immediately after the prayer and reflection, someone— usually one of the ministry leaders—shares their story—either a coming-out or a parent story. Then the next person to the right or left tells their story and so on until everyone in the circle has had the opportunity to speak. While everyone has a space to share, more time is given to those who are there for the first time, as they tend to be the ones in active crisis and may need more time to share what they are going through. Everyone listens without judgment and follows the pastoral care principles outlined above—being a listening Church, a Church of encounter, and a Church of accompaniment. Often, those members who have been there the longest spend less time telling their story so that those who are new and in distress have more time to speak. The meetings usually last about one and a half hours. At the end, ministry leaders usually close with a prayer and the meeting is adjourned. The leaders often bring coffee or cookies to share at the end of the meeting, allowing people to mingle and connect with others.

Advantages

The biggest advantage of the support group model is that it requires little resources and is easier to lead and to organize. There is typically a monthly meeting that does not require exhaustive planning efforts. The most effort involves planning an opening reflection and finding prayers that are reflective of people's lived experience. Leaders are also encouraged to be aware of any current events affecting LGBTQ persons.[3]

Disadvantages

The biggest disadvantage is that this model is not the best if one wants the ministry to grow in numbers. In other words, people who come in distress often attend the meetings once or twice, but once the crisis has passed, those people often

---

3. For sample prayers used by existing LGBTQ ministries, see appendix C.

stop attending. One reason why they stop attending is because these inclusive ministries tend to be rare, so people often must travel distances to attend them. With a few exceptions, people are less likely to drive long distances once the crisis has passed. Therefore, these ministries are usually small ministries of five to ten regular attendants.

Another factor is that a monthly meeting can sometimes be a disadvantage, especially for those who really need community. For community building it is recommended that these LGBTQ ministries plan social events or other activities in addition to their monthly meeting.

DID YOU KNOW?

Pastors need to be aware that these ministries tend to be smaller. When Cynthia started *Agape*, she always found it difficult when the yearly parish fiesta was approaching, because all the ministries were asked to sell a certain number of raffle tickets to fundraise for the parish, regardless of the size of their ministry. While a ministry of forty to fifty people might have no problem selling tickets, asking the same of smaller support group ministries was a challenge, especially if members were experiencing some crises of their own.

Evangelization Model

The evangelization model is organized very differently from the support group model.

Characteristics

LGBTQ groups that follow the evangelization model usually meet once a week, as opposed to once a month. Their meeting format is very similar to the format of young adult ministries or other prayer groups. On regular days, they may start with fifteen or twenty minutes of songs of worship—if they have a choir or someone who can lead in worship—which is followed by a prayer or Scripture reflection, and then a guest speaker who speaks on a predetermined subject for forty-five minutes to an hour. These meetings also usually close with a prayer.

While the focus in these groups is still on pastoral care, there is also a focus on general evangelization and religious formation, that is, teaching group members more about Jesus, the gospel, doctrine, Church feasts, and a myriad of other topics. Mostly, the focus is on creating an unconditional, welcoming space where group members can have a deeper encounter with Jesus, with themselves, and with their faith.

Advantages

The main advantage of this evangelization model is that it allows for a greater sense of community because members do not have to wait a month for the next meeting, and they see each other regularly. These ministries are usually better attended and are more active in the parish. For those ministries with more resources, they may even have yearly or biannual spiritual retreats. At best, they can be a great space for spiritual growth, a deep sense of community, and friendship.

Disadvantages

One of the main disadvantages of this evangelization model is that it offers less space for listening—less space for someone who is going through a deep crisis to talk about what is happening in their life. Because the focus is on evangelization, most of the activities focus on teaching rather than on pastoral care. Only after deep friendships are forged can these ministries be places for personalized support.

Another disadvantage is that a ministry that follows the evangelization model requires more resources and planning than a support group. Consequently, they must be led either by a paid staff member or a group of volunteers (a leadership table), who leads the group for a fixed period without pay (e.g., a two-year volunteer commitment). The leadership table must commit to planning ministry events, weekly meetings, retreats, fundraising, and other activities. Ministries that follow the evangelization model usually thrive in parishes with a supportive parish community, but not so much in parishes where the community is not open to the ministry.

Another disadvantage is that these ministries often have difficulty finding guest speakers who are aware of the need for pastoral care, are well-informed about LGBTQ science and social issues, are inclusive in their approach, and have appropriate religious formation and/or pastoral experience in LGBTQ ministry. Because the focus of these ministries is on evangelization and religious formation, they often struggle figuring out what topics should be included in the ministry's curriculum so that they offer appropriate pastoral care that is inclusive and welcoming while remaining within the directives of Church doctrine.

In considering an appropriate curriculum for LGBTQ ministries, other non-LGBTQ ministries can be helpful. For instance, most young adult groups provide an integral formation to sustain all aspects of the self, not just topics of sexuality. Such a curriculum includes topics that help the person grow in their self-knowledge and their knowledge of Jesus and Church doctrine, and that help participants put their faith into acts of mercy or justice.[4] An integral formation program fosters self-growth as well as a growth in a spiritual life that considers the whole person as a child of God. These ministries will also focus on teaching others how to be a listening Church, a Church of encounter, and a Church of accompaniment.

How to Start a Parish Ministry

While each parish community is different and there is no single formula for starting a successful parish ministry, the following four steps are a helpful guide.

Step 1: Identify the Need

It is important to ask yourself if there is a need in your parish community for an LGBTQ ministry. If you or a family member is an LGBTQ Catholic or a parent of an LGBTQ Catholic, there is a need. If you know someone in the parish community who is an LGBTQ Catholic or a parent of an LGBTQ Catholic, there is a need. The moment two or more people in the parish community have the same need, then a ministry is born. Discuss the possibility of creating a ministry together and whether each of you would be willing to share your story with your pastor or parish life director to create an awareness of the need.

Step 2: Reach Out to Other Existing Ministries

Based on their pastoral experience, existing ministries can provide guidance and a wealth of knowledge and advice regarding the best practices in starting and continuing a ministry. The problem is that most existing parish or diocesan ministries are

---

4. Such topics might include self-esteem, Church feasts, talents or God-given gifts, topics of self-growth, social justice, the seven cardinal virtues, chastity, Mary, LGBTQ history and issues, prayer, professional and religious vocations, conflict resolution, forgiveness, discernment, and the saints.

accustomed to doing their work in private and most of them have either not written down what they know or are hard to contact. Whenever possible, call an existing ministry and set up a time when you can speak by phone; these ministries are very important resources.

Step 3: Plan a Meeting with Your Pastor

It is important to plan a meeting with your pastor, including what will be addressed and the format of the meeting. It can be helpful to begin the meeting by sharing your personal story without discussing doctrine, as the focus must first be on creating awareness of the need and on putting the wounds of this part of the Body of Christ at the center of the dialogue. This should be a talk from heart to heart.

Once an awareness of the need is at the center of the meeting, you can present some ideas as to what a ministry would look like. This might include what other existing ministries have done, presenting sample mission statements and approaches, explaining the need for pastoral care, and voicing your own vision and mission for the ministry.[5]

At this point, you may also have to address any questions or concerns your pastor might have. It is very likely that your pastor will want to address Church doctrine, which is discussed in the next chapter and can help you prepare for this conversation. Listen to your pastor while reminding him that the purpose of the ministry is first and foremost to offer pastoral care.

In advance of your meeting, gather resources that might be helpful to your pastor, such as documents written by the bishops (in the United States, the USCCB), books, articles, and resources provided by other LGBTQ ministries.

---

5. For sample mission/vision statements of existing LGBTQ ministries, see appendix B.

Step 4: Invite a Companion

When meeting with the pastor, we recommend inviting two or more people interested in creating this ministry to attend. Sometimes members of existing ministries in your area might be willing to go with you so they are available to respond to any questions your pastor may have about the ministry in their parish community. But remember, you know your parish community better than anyone else, so you are still the person leading the meeting. Share your stories, share your ministry plan, and if needed, address any concerns.

What If the Pastor Says No?

The most important thing one can have when starting a ministry is the support of the pastor. If he does not support ministry efforts, keep sharing your story with him and others—if you are emotionally ready and if it is safe to do so.

What If the Pastor Says Yes?

At this point you will have to create a plan for the ministry. Determine whether you will meet on Church property or in a private home, whether your ministry will be a ministry for LGBTQ persons or for parents of LGBTQ children, whether you will follow the support group model or the evangelization model, create a name (e.g., "Always Our Children," "GLO" [Gay Lesbian Outreach], "Agape," "No Barriers to Christ," "Courageous Hearts," "One Table"), develop a mission statement, plan a kick-off event, figure out advertising and social media for your ministry, and invite others to join.

What If the Pastor Says Yes, but the Community Opposes It?

The best person to create awareness with the parish community is the pastor. Without his support, it will be difficult to have an inclusive ministry in a hostile community.

It is important to get involved in the community, let others know what your ministry is about, participate in parish festivals and events, plan activities, prayer nights, presentations, and invite other ministries. People are afraid of what they do not know. Befriend others. Educate and create awareness regarding the need for pastoral care.

If, even after sharing stories there is no support, perhaps consider a neighboring parish where the need is acknowledged and combine efforts there.

DIOCESAN/ARCHDIOCESAN MINISTRIES

Purpose and Mission

Most diocesan/archdiocesan ministries have a three-pronged purpose: pastoral care, diocesan-wide religious formation, and outreach.

Pastoral Care

While in parish ministry, pastoral care of the individual is the primary purpose of LGBTQ ministry, in the case of diocesan/archdiocesan ministries, the primary purpose is to model to parish ministries how to accompany each other unconditionally. For example, some archdiocesan ministries have monthly gatherings where they invite the leaders of LGBTQ parish ministries so that they may get to meet each other and plan or participate in events together. This is helpful because parish ministries often feel isolated and as if they are the only parish in the diocese offering LGBTQ ministry. These spaces are often welcoming and inclusive. However, the mission of diocesan/archdiocesan ministries goes beyond that, as they also provide guidance to parish ministries and lead other diocesan efforts.[6]

Characteristics

There are a few Catholic dioceses and archdioceses worldwide that have created diocesan or archdiocesan LGBTQ ministries. The Catholic Ministry with Lesbian and Gay Persons of the Archdiocese of Los Angeles and the Ministry to Families and Friends with Gay and Lesbian Catholics of the Diocese of San Bernardino are just two examples.

The characteristics of these ministries can vary depending on the diocese. For instance, in some dioceses, a paid staff member leads the ministry while in other dioceses the ministry is led by volunteer lay ministers along with the ministry's spiritual director—usually a priest. Diocesan ministries sometimes have an office at the diocesan building, or they may be hosted by a particular parish but listed on the diocesan website as an official ministry.

Whatever the form, the main characteristic is that these ministries are often created by bishops or archbishops, rather than laypersons or others. It is my hope that bishops who have created these ministries or are discerning whether to do so may communicate with their fellow bishops regarding some best practices. Each diocese/archdiocese must consider the specific needs and characteristics of their regions. For instance, for American dioceses, the creation of these ministries is a life issue

---

6. For samples of Diocesan/Archdiocesan ministry mission statements, see appendix B.

in that it prevents suicides, bullying, and other losses of life. In contrast, in other parts of the world, the creation of these ministries is a life issue when state-sponsored homophobia—the criminalization of LGBTQ persons or even death penalty—is commonplace.[7] For this reason, the form the ministry takes is not as important as its purpose.

Religious Formation and Guidance

Some diocesan and archdiocesan ministries have become the hubs of religious formation on LGBTQ issues for all the parishes in their diocese. Those who minister at the diocesan/ archdiocesan level are often invited to speak at different religious formation events or parishes about our experience in LGBTQ ministry, the need for such ministry, the basics of Church doctrine, and other relevant topics.

They also offer guidance to those wishing to start a ministry at the parish level and can offer advice and support on pastoral care and best practices to priests, religious, and laypersons in the diocese.

Outreach

Often included in diocesan ministries are outreach activities, which are usually either *internal* or *outreach on the margins*. In this sense, the form of outreach can range anywhere from simply becoming visible in church spaces to going out of church environments even *to the margins*. One way to become visible in church spaces is having a ministry booth and passing out flyers at diocesan/archdiocesan or even parish events. Another option is to hold an annual Pride Mass for LGBTQ Catholics and their families or a Mass of belonging and welcome for all those

---

7. See ILGA World—the International Lesbian, Gay, Bisexual, Trans and Intersex Association map on sexual orientation laws: https://ilga.org/maps-sexual-orientation-laws (accessed September 15, 2021).

who have felt rejected by the Church. Internal outreach activities include not only reaching out to LGBTQ Catholics but also building bridges with church leaders. Diocesan ministries might meet once a year with their bishop or archbishop to build such bridges.

Some ministries go beyond internal outreach activities by bringing the Church to the margins. For instance, the archdiocesan ministry in Los Angeles—the Catholic Ministry with Lesbian and Gay Persons (CMLGP)—regularly has a booth at multiple Pride parades in the County of Los Angeles. While the ministry has been criticized for its presence at these parades, the booth provides a loving, welcoming, and accepting presence for many LGBTQ people there. Often, some people think that the booth is there to *convert* them to heterosexuality; others cannot believe the booth is affiliated with *the* Catholic Church. Mostly, however, people are extremely grateful and pleasantly surprised to see the booth present. It provides the opportunity to *encounter* the pain that the LGBTQ community has experienced from religions and to bring the gospel of love to the margins without any agenda.

More recently, CMLGP has started to participate in the Models of Pride Conference. This is the world's largest conference on LGBTQ issues and is usually held annually at a college campus in the United States. The conference has three main tracks: a parent, a youth, and a professional track. Some of the workshops offered are also faith-based. While the CMLGP has only participated so far by having a booth, the ministry hopes to offer workshops there in the future.

Building Bridges with the Bishops

Whenever I give a workshop on LGBTQ ministry, I am often asked, "How can I help my bishop start an LGBTQ ministry?" The response is complicated because each diocese has its own context and culture, but we each have the task of building bridges between the LGBTQ community and the Church. Certainly, sharing our story with our bishops and fostering friendship and dialogue is helpful. It is important to create awareness for the need of the ministry with our bishops, but we must also encounter each person where they are. This applies to our bishops as much as it applies to anyone else. As laypersons, it is essential to grow in personal faith, to learn more about best practices in LGBTQ ministry, and then, if our bishop seeks help in shaping safe spaces for this ministry, being available to assist.

RELIGIOUS ORDERS

Ministries operated by religious orders can vary in organizational structure and format. Therefore, rather than characterizing them into one group, the following are some examples. This is not an exhaustive list, as there are many examples where religious orders are ministering to LGBTQ Catholics.

The Marianists

The Society of Mary, also known as the Marianists, a two-hundred-year-old Catholic religious congregation of brothers and priests, the Marianist Sisters, and the Marianist Lay Community have a strong LGBTQ ministry. The LGBT Initiative, a team of the Marianist Social Justice Collaborative, responds to the Church's call to be welcoming and compassionate by offering pastoral care and spiritual support for LGBTQ Catholics and their families and by fostering dialogue, education, and understanding among the diverse communities and institutions affiliated with the Society of Mary.[8]

Among the many activities the Initiative offers, there is an annual spiritual retreat each November in Menlo Park, California,

---

8. "LGBT Initiative," Marianist Social Justice Collaborative, website, accessed November 4, 2020, https://msjc.net/lgbt-initiative.

called "A Beloved Community of Saints" that has become popular for LGBTQ Catholics from all parts of the United States.

The Franciscans

The Franciscan San Damiano Retreat House in Danville, California, also holds an annual spiritual retreat for transgender Catholics.[9] The goal of the retreat "You Are Wonderfully Made: Welcome and Respect for Transgender Individuals and Their Families" led by Deacon Raymond Dever is to reflect on how the Church can better minister to and welcome transgender people and their families. The program includes opportunities to reflect on the experience of the transgender person or a loved one who is transgender.

The Society of Jesus (Jesuits)

Many of us are familiar with Jesuit father James Martin and his book *Building a Bridge.* Through his book, Fr. Martin has started an extremely important dialogue about the need to build a bridge between the Catholic Church and the LGBTQ community and vice versa. In addition to Fr. Martin's ministry, the Society of Jesus has often been at the forefront in ministry, whether it is at Jesuit Catholic universities, in their parishes, or other apostolates.

HIGHER EDUCATION

Ministry to LGBTQ Catholics in higher education can also vary in organizational structure and format. These ministries

9. "San Damiano Retreat," The Franciscan Friars, website, accessed November 8, 2020, https://sandamiano.org. See also "You Are Wonderfully Made," The Franciscan Friars, accessed November 8, 2020, https://sandamiano.org/wp-content/uploads/2019/05/2020-June-Deacon-Ray-Dever-Weekend2.pdf.

can be found at both private and public institutions of higher education. In public institutions, they are often supported by and based at the institution's Catholic Newman Center. For instance, the St. Thomas Aquinas Catholic Newman Community, serving the University of Nevada-Las Vegas (UNLV) campus, is home to Imago Dei, a Catholic LGBTQ ministry and an independent 501(c)(3) religious nonprofit organization. The ministry is led by a Board of Directors under the direction of the pastor of the St. Thomas Aquinas Newman Center at UNLV.

The ministry was established to support LGBTQ Catholics and their families and loved ones. It is a place for those persons who have persevered in their faith but also for those who long to return, as well as "for families and friends who want to understand, love, and support their loved ones who are LGBTQ—especially through the light of their Catholic faith."[10]

CATHOLIC HIGH SCHOOLS

There are several Catholic high schools in the United States that have created safe spaces for their LGBTQ students and their families. Because our focus is not on high school ministry, I recommend the book *Creating Safe Environments for LGBT Students: A Catholic Schools Perspective*. Based on five years of pilot testing in Catholic schools, it emphasizes safe-staff training in integrating the Church's pastoral, social, and moral dimensions with the special needs of LGBTQ students.[11]

---

10. "Imago Dei," website, accessed November 4, 2020, https://imagodeilv.wixsite .com/home.

11. Michael J. Bayly, *Creating Safe Environments for LGBT Students: A Catholic Schools Perspective* (New York: Routledge, 2012).

NATIONAL MINISTRIES

When thinking of Catholic ministries or organizations that have a national reach beyond their individual diocese or archdiocese or even their state, two ministries come to mind: Fortunate Families and New Ways Ministry. Both ministries began before it was popular or even *acceptable* and, over time, have offered very valuable resources and guidance. This section is not an exhaustive list, and it is focused on ministries in the United States. National ministries may also exist in other countries.

Fortunate Families

Fortunate Families is an organization based in the Diocese of Lexington, Kentucky, that focuses on ministry with parents at a national level.[12] It was founded in 2004 by Casey and Mary Ellen Lopata, the parents of four children, including a son who came out to them as gay at the age of nineteen. The Lopatas have worked in ministry with gay and lesbian Catholics and their families since 1992 and were consulters to the National Conference of Catholic Bishops' Committee on Marriage and the Family in preparing the document, "Always Our Children: A Pastoral Message to Parents of Homosexual Children and Suggestions for Pastoral Ministers," issued in September 1997. The Lopatas retired from the Fortunate Families board in 2014 after guiding and growing the organization through its first decade, though they continue to serve on the organization's advisory council.

Fortunate Families continues to do great work supporting LGBTQ Catholics, their families, and allies by facilitating conversation and "sharing personal stories within dioceses, parishes

---

12. "Fortunate Families," website, accessed January 8, 2019, https://fortunate families.com.

and communities, especially with bishops, pastors and Church leadership."[13] As such, their focus is not only on accompaniment but also in providing resources for anyone who wishes to start a parent ministry or an LGBTQ ministry in the United States or the world, as well as build bridges with church leadership.

New Ways Ministry

New Ways Ministry is a nonprofit organization devoted to LGBTQ Catholic concerns.[14] The ministry was founded in 1977 by Fr. Robert Nugent, SDS, and Sr. Jeannine Gramick, SL (previously SSND). The organization's name was inspired by words in the 1976 pastoral letter "Sexuality: God's Gift," written by Bishop Francis J. Mugavero of Brooklyn, New York. Just like its name and the organization's cofounders, "the vision and philosophy of this group was solidly Catholic," but they faced some opposition. In 1984, the Vatican required that the cofounders separate themselves from New Ways Ministry. The cofounders have continued their ministry to gay and lesbian Catholics with the knowledge of the Vatican under the auspices of their religious orders. Despite all the challenges, New Ways Ministry has continued its work as "bridge-builders... reaching out, in one direction, to gay and lesbian people, and, in the other direction, to people working within the Church and Church structures."

After more than forty years of service and ministry, New Ways Ministry continues its pioneering and prophetic bridge-building work in offering resources, including a daily blog, a listing of some welcoming parishes, colleges, and spiritual retreats for LGBTQ Catholics and others.

---

13. "Fortunate Families," website.
14. "New Ways Ministry," website, accessed on January 8, 2019, https://www.newwaysministry.org.

INTERNATIONAL MINISTRIES

The following ministries have a direct, international outreach. It is difficult to classify them under the same category because their history, approaches to the ministry, and relationship to the global Church are different. Please note that other ministries that are not listed here may exist.

Global Network of Rainbow Catholics

The Global Network of Rainbow Catholics (GNRC) "brings together organizations and individuals who work for pastoral care and justice for [LGBTQ Catholics] and their families."[15] The GNRC was "founded in October 2015...to date, the GNRC represents 25 groups of LGBTQI Catholics, their families and friends from all continents....[GNRC] works for inclusion, dignity, and equality of this community in the Roman Catholic Church and society."[16] The GNRC comprises various levels and types of ministries, including some members that act on an individual capacity.

Dignity

Dignity is a ministry founded in 1969 by Fr. Patrick X. Nidorf, OSA, an Augustinian priest and psychologist. In the beginning, Dignity's position and purpose was explicitly at odds with some parts of Church doctrine.[17] By 1971, the then-Archbishop Timothy

---

15. "GRNC Mission, Ethos & Values," Global Network of Rainbow Catholics website, accessed January 10, 2020, https://rainbowcatholics.org/mission-ethos-values/.

16. "Global Network of Rainbow Catholics," website, accessed January 10, 2020, http://rainbowcatholics.org.

17. From as early as the 1970s, the first draft of Dignity's "Statement of Position and Purpose" included the following: "We believe that homosexuality is a natural variation on the use of sex. It implies no sickness or immorality. Those with such sexual orientation have a natural right to use their power of sex in a way that is

Manning forbid Fr. Nidorf to have anything to do with the group. Fr. Nidorf resigned. Dignity members continued doing their work but continued facing opposition. In 1986 and 1987, Dignity chapters were evicted from all Church property.[18]

While Dignity's history has been rockier than that of others, it is important to recognize that Dignity has been doing prophetic work by serving part of the Body of Christ that would have left the Church long ago by offering a safe space for members to nurture a relationship with Jesus and the Church.

Courage/Encourage

Courage is an international apostolate of the Catholic Church that ministers to persons with "same-sex attractions."[19] Similarly, Encourage is an apostolate for "parents, spouses, siblings, and friends of people who identify as LGBTQ." These ministries have had the full support of the Catholic Church since inception and have been a helpful resource and space for some LGBTQ Catholics; while for others, the spaces offered by these ministries have not been welcoming enough.

Courage's mission and methods have evolved over the years. Courage was formed in the early 1980s as a *spiritual support group*, which would assist gay Catholics in adhering to the teachings of the Church on sexuality and sexual behavior. Currently, the mission of Courage has five goals: (1) to live chaste lives; (2) to dedicate their lives to Christ; (3) to foster a spirit of fellowship; (4) to be mindful of the truth that chaste friendships are possible and necessary; and (5) to live lives that may

---

both responsible and fulfilling... and should use it with a sense of pride." While the understanding of sexual orientation has developed over time, in the 1970s this was a revolutionary statement coming from a Church ministry. See "DignityUSA," website, accessed September 15, 2021, https://www.dignityusa.org.

18. "DignityUSA," website, accessed January 12, 2020.

19. "Courage International," website, accessed January 12, 2020, https://couragerc .org.

serve as a role model. To help people remain abstinent from sex, Courage uses a twelve-step program, like the model used in Alcoholics Anonymous (AA). Courage does not currently support conversion therapy, but that has not always been the case. Conversion therapy has been proven ineffective and harmful[20] and has been fully or partially banned in more than twenty-five states.[21]

While some LGBTQ Catholics have found the space offered by the Courage apostolate helpful, whether permanently or temporarily, a great majority of LGBTQ Catholics who have seen Courage as the only option in ministry, have left the Church as a result and often mention that they felt Courage was not a safe or healthy space.

In my opinion, Courage's predominant focus on sex can make members feel very uncomfortable. For example, just because someone is an LGBTQ Catholic does not mean that they are sexually active or in a romantic relationship. Even if a person is in a relationship, this does not mean that they have difficulty controlling their sexual impulses or that they have sexual addictions that require a twelve-step program. People need to be treated as a full human being, not just a sexual being. (I have historically experienced my orientation primarily as a romantic emotional connection, more than a sexual one, so this hyper focus on sexuality is irrelevant and highly uncomfortable.)

Many LGBTQ Catholics who are seeking to join a ministry are often looking for a community where they can nurture their relationship with Jesus, learn more about Jesus and the gospel, and find a safe space for life discernment. As noted

---

20. What We Know Project, Cornell University, "What Does the Scholarly Research Say about Whether Conversion Therapy Can Alter Sexual Orientation Without Causing Harm?" (online literature review), 2016, https://whatweknow.inequality.cornell.edu.

21. "Conversion 'Therapy' Laws," Movement Advancement Project, website, accessed September 15, 2021, https://www.lgbtmap.org/equality-maps/conversion _therapy.

earlier, this space is essential for our spiritual and personal development and to build a solid foundation.

While sexuality is part of everyone's life, albeit an important one, it is only one aspect of us. LGBTQ Catholics still have the same needs as other Catholics and still need to grow in other aspects of their lives and in spirituality. For instance, in young adult ministry, the members receive a full, integral faith formation that considers their whole being. I remember attending young adult ministry meetings when I was younger and being excited because at every meeting, we would talk about different topics that helped me become a better person and deepen my faith. While we did talk about chastity as part of the curriculum, the focus was on integral spiritual and personal growth. If those meetings had been exclusively or primarily about chastity, I doubt I would have continued attending because, while I believe that chastity is a beautiful and a very important doctrine and its knowledge and practice is necessary and beautiful, what I needed was to grow in my faith, to grow in relationship with Jesus, and to be treated as a full human being. Similar integrated programs are needed to welcome LGBTQ Catholics to any ministry.

Nevertheless, there are people, both LGBTQ and heterosexual persons, who would benefit from a Catholic twelve-step program to help them with any sexual addictions. The fact that such an important and helpful twelve-step model is only targeting LGBTQ persons and not available to heterosexual persons is both prejudicial and discriminatory for both groups; it prevents this important tool from reaching others in the heterosexual community who may need it.

There are some positive aspects to the approach that Courage takes. For instance, its focus on fellowship and in creating a space of holy friendships is attractive. Some LGBTQ Catholics really enjoy that aspect of the apostolate and find peace in being able to remain abstinent while having a community of mutual support in their discernment process. Inclusive LGBTQ ministries also offer similar spaces, though not as an implicit condition for membership. Those thinking of starting an LGBTQ ministry are encouraged to be aware of this need.

Another positive aspect of Courage is its focus on members dedicating their lives to Christ and in service to others, as well as living lives that can be role models for others. Inclusive LGBTQ ministries also offer this space, and we hope to continue dedicating our lives in service to others and growing in relationship with Jesus and the Church.

Regardless of what ministry a person finds attractive, it is essential to remember that we are all part of the same Body of Christ.

Finally, many LGBTQ Catholics feel comfortable with the approach of Courage and find peace with the term "Catholic with same-sex attraction." Others, however, find peace in using the umbrella term "Queer" or "LGBTQ Catholic" and not having to identify with one orientation or another. Ministers in LGBTQ ministry need to be aware of and respect this reality.

4

THE BASICS OF
CHURCH DOCTRINE[1]

The principles of our Catholic faith and doctrine stem from three sources: Tradition (the revealed Word of God in history); Scripture (the Bible, the written record); and the Magisterium (the pope and the bishops).[2] Catholic doctrine that applies to LGBTQ Catholics can be divided into three main categories:

1. Dignity of the Human Person
2. Discrimination
3. Chastity

DIGNITY OF THE HUMAN PERSON

All people are created in the image and likeness of God and thus possess innate human dignity that must be acknowledged and respected. . . .

---

1. This chapter focuses on Church doctrine as it applies to LGBTQ Catholics and is not a comprehensive discussion. There are many great Catholic writers who have done an excellent job in explaining the doctrine. My task, here, is to provide an overall summary of the main points of established Church doctrine, highlighting the elements that are often ignored when speaking about LGBTQ issues, and starting a dialogue to promote pastoral sensitivity in areas where the teachings are often interpreted as being discriminatory. This chapter is intended to be accessible and written primarily from my perspective as a Catholic and as a coordinator of Religious Education programs.

2. *Catechism of the Catholic Church* (CCC), §§74–100, accessed September 17, 2021, https://www.vatican.va/archive/ENG0015/_INDEX.HTM.

[Homosexual persons] must be accepted with respect, compassion, and sensitivity.

Catechism of the Catholic Church (CCC),
§§1700–1702, 2358

This child, who has always been God's gift to you, may now be the cause of another gift: your family becoming more honest, respectful, and supportive.

USCCB, "Always Our Children," 1997

The dignity of the human person is a cornerstone of Catholic social teaching. All human beings are created in God's image and likeness regardless of race, sex, age, national origin, religion, sexual orientation, employment or economic status, health, intelligence, achievement, or any other differentiating characteristic.[3] Any differentiating characteristic makes absolutely no difference in terms of each person's inherent dignity, the dignity that we are born with by virtue of being children of God. We are all made in God's image and likeness (*imago Dei*), and we have an inherent dignity that must be respected. This teaching includes sexual orientation or gender identity, for it applies to *all* persons.

Application

Applying this teaching of the *dignity of the human person* centers on the word *person*. There have been countless instances—such as slavery, genocide, attacks on specific racial or religious groups, and against immigrants, and so on—where the dignity of a person or group of persons has been violated. Each of these historical events demonstrate that injustice is

---

3. See Robert P. Maloney, "Ten Foundational Principles in the Social Teaching of the Church," *Vincentiana* 43, no. 3 (1999), https://via.library.depaul.edu/vincentiana/vol43/iss3/1/.

often preceded by a characterization of "the other" as "less than persons." For this reason, the gap between the theory and the practice of treating others with dignity needs to be bridged by focusing on the "person" and what it means to be treated as such.

We cannot treat LGBTQ persons with dignity unless we treat them as persons, full human beings made in the image and likeness of God and born with an inherent dignity that must be respected. We are all more than just our sexual orientation, identity, race, religion, or any other characteristic. LGBTQ persons are full persons, children of God born with God-given gifts, with the capacity for self-knowledge and self-determination, with virtues and shortcomings, life goals and spiritual yearnings, interests and needs beyond sexual orientation, born with an identity and in community, and with full dignity that must be respected. We must see LGBTQ Catholics as people—our brothers and sisters—who are also part of the Body of Christ. This is paramount in practice if we are to follow this important part of the teaching.

LGBTQ persons are dehumanized when their lives and life experiences are framed solely as a political agenda, or even worse, when we equate them with the dawn of some "evil force" or "apocalyptic future." We should not dehumanize LGBTQ persons; we must never reduce people to less than who they are.

What does it mean to see LGBTQ persons as persons? Let's consider Jesus, who was both human and divine (CCC 464). As a human being, he was born within a specific geographical, historical, political, religious, and cultural context. Just like us, Jesus was immersed in the cultural context of his time (§472), a cultural context where many groups of people were seen as less than persons. (The most common examples we encounter in the Gospels include women, those who were considered sinners, and those with illnesses.) One reason why Jesus attracted followers was that he saw people, first and foremost, in their full humanity.

Consider, for example, Jesus's encounter with the Samaritan woman (John 4:3–15). While on his way to Galilee, Jesus stopped at a town in Samaria to get some rest, as he was tired from his journey. He sat down by a well around noontime. Then a Samaritan woman came to draw water from the well where Jesus was sitting, and Jesus started a conversation with her. Note, here, that Jesus had a conversation with the Samaritan woman. This, in and of itself, was revolutionary.

In Jesus's time women were not treated as persons. Furthermore, they did not have the full legal rights that came with *personhood status* such as property rights, right to self-determination and autonomy, and so on.[4] A man in the Jewish world did not usually speak with a woman in public, not even with his own wife. It was even more culturally unacceptable for a man to speak with a woman privately. Yet Jesus saw this person in front of him and started a simple conversation, a dialogue with someone who, in addition to being a woman, was considered a "sinful woman."[5] Notice that this conversation was not a sermon, and it was not a one-sided monologue, it was a dialogue between two people. Furthermore, Jesus approached this woman not from a position of power or as Son of God, but from his own human need; he asked her for a favor, *Will you give me a drink?* She was absolutely surprised and astonished by the very fact that this man was speaking to her. As Pope John Paul II notes,

---

4. A woman was almost always under the protection and authority of a man: her father, her husband, or a male relative of her husband if she was a widow. They had little access to property or inheritance, except through a male relative. Any money a woman earned belonged to her husband. Men could legally divorce a woman for almost any reason, simply by handing her a writ of divorce. A woman, however, could not divorce her husband.

5. John Paul II, apostolic letter *Mulieris Dignitatem*, On the Dignity and Vocation of Women on the Occasion of the Marian Year, August 15, 1988, §§12, 15, http://www.vatican.va.

This is an unprecedented event, if one remembers the usual way women were treated by those who were teachers [of religious law] in Israel; whereas in Jesus of Nazareth's way of acting such an event becomes normal.[6]

In addition to being a woman, she was also a Samaritan. In Jesus's time Jews did not associate with Samaritans, and Jesus was Jewish. Yet Jesus didn't reduce her to her gender nor to her ethnicity, rather he saw the *person* in front of him. By opening a dialogue with her, he refused to treat her as any less than a full person, he treated her with dignity and raised that dignity by becoming her friend.

Jesus's actions were a challenge to the religious and social rules of his time, prioritizing love and uplifting those on the margins. Jesus came to show us the way. This encounter was transformative for the Samaritan woman and is, in part, what motivated her to drink the living water that Jesus offered. This radical love and inclusiveness are what motivated her to become an apostle, a witness to Jesus's mission of love to other Samaritans. The key to Jesus's ministry and model of encounter is found in his perceiving and treating persons as persons.

As disciples of Jesus, our utmost desire in life must be to follow Jesus; nothing else but this will ever quench our thirst. Jesus showed us the way to treat others with dignity. Seeing the human being in front of us while setting aside prejudice and preconceived ideas, can be a transformative experience for all of us, for those giving and for those receiving. This is the first part of Church doctrine that applies to LGBTQ persons that is often ignored by many Catholics and not stressed enough.

---

6. John Paul II, *Mulieris Dignitatem*, §15.

Tips for Applying This Teaching

There are ways that we can respect the dignity of the LGBTQ person and assist others to do the same:

As individuals. Catholics must not be afraid to befriend LGBTQ persons and such friendship must be genuine with no hidden agendas.

As educators, and catechists. Those who teach in religious education programs, laypersons who regularly preach in ministries, and all others in positions of leadership have a duty to educate themselves fully about this topic if they are to guide others in the faith.

As pastors and ministers. In considering what curriculum is appropriate for LGBTQ ministries, treat LGBTQ persons as full persons. Integral formation programs/curriculums that consider the whole person and that are not exclusively focused on sexuality should be highly encouraged.

For everyone. We must all learn to be a listening Church, a Church of accompaniment, and a Church of encounter with LGBTQ persons, walking together on our journey of faith regardless of what that journey looks like.

HARASSMENT, DISCRIMINATION, HATRED, AND VIOLENCE AGAINST HOMOSEXUAL PERSONS MUST *NOT* BE TOLERATED

All homosexual persons have a right to be welcomed into the community, to hear the word of God, and to receive pastoral care...[and] should have opportunities to lead and serve the community.

USCCB, "Always Our Children," 1997

It is deplorable that homosexual persons have been and are objects of violent malice in speech or in action. Such treatment deserves condemnation from the Church's pastors wherever it occurs.

Congregation for the Doctrine of the Faith, "On the
Pastoral Care of Homosexual Persons," 1986

Homosexuals, like everyone else, should not suffer from prejudice against their basic human rights. They have a right to respect, friendship, and justice. They should have an active role in the Christian community.

National Conference of Catholic Bishops,
"To Live in Christ Jesus," 1976

The second category of Church doctrine that applies to LGBTQ Catholics is that harassment, discrimination, hatred, and violence against homosexual persons must not be tolerated. This is a clear and well-established principle, but we often fail in practicing it.

To illustrate this point, on June 12, 2016, a man went into the Pulse Nightclub, a gay venue in Orlando, Florida, and started shooting people, killing forty-nine persons and wounding fifty-three. This was an attack that, unlike other general mass shootings, specifically targeted the LGBTQ community. It is the deadliest incident in the history of violence against LGBTQ people and, at the time, the deadliest mass shooting by a single gunman in the United States.

On the day of the shooting, I remember receiving calls from many of my LGBTQ Catholic friends who reside in different parts of the country. Each of us expressed how deeply saddened we felt because we were reminded that the LGBTQ community is still very vulnerable, even in a developed country like ours.

Toward the end of the following day, which was a Sunday, I was getting even more calls from my LGBTQ Catholic friends asking such questions as these: "Why is it that in my parish the shooting wasn't even mentioned or talked about during mass?" "Why is it that prayers for the dead and wounded were not even included in the universal prayer?" "Why is it that in many parishes, no one even acknowledged what happened?" "Why did so few bishops make any public statements about this incident?" At my parish, we did have a special prayer, but my parish was one of a few. Everywhere else it was as if nothing had happened, as if the LBGTQ community was invisible.

On Monday morning, I posted a prayer on some of my social media channels, a prayer for the souls of those who were killed and for the recovery of those who were wounded at the Orlando shooting. As the week went by, my LGBTQ Catholic friends and I grew depressed as we read the online responses to our prayer requests—responses coming from fellow parishioners, ministers, and others who are highly respected and super involved in our parishes and in Catholic media. The responses included the following: "Well, they got what they deserved!" "It was their choice to die." "They put the noose around their own neck." "They had to face the consequences of their own sin." Such responses were heartbreaking. This was, at best, a show of ignorance of doctrine, and at worst, deeply immoral and troubling, and surely, a failure of religious education on this topic.

The victims of the Orlando shooting were killed for no reason. The persons who were killed did not choose nor deserve to die. Catholic doctrine is very clear on this matter. We must not tolerate violence.

In their 2006 pastoral letter, "Ministry to Persons with a Homosexual Inclination: Guidelines for Pastoral Care," the United States Conference of Catholic Bishops (USCCB) stated, "We recognize that these persons have been, and often continue to be objects of scorn, hatred, and even violence in some sectors of our society. Sometimes this hatred is manifested clearly; other times, it is masked and gives rise to more disguised forms of hatred."

Many of the negative responses to the Orlando shooting from fellow Catholics are a disguised form of hatred, even if those responsible are not aware of it.

I would love to say that this was a one-time incident, but ever since I have started being publicly involved in LGBTQ ministry, I have faced similar responses coming from Catholic individuals who believe their response to me is what the Church requires of them. I have been told that I am going to burn in the fire of hell, that God despises me, that I am a shame, among other things. As a Church, we must do a better job of educating people about the gravity of this kind of attitude and about the doctrine regarding this matter.

The USCCB also made the following call in the 1991 letter, "Human Sexuality: A Catholic Perspective for Education and Lifelong Learning":

> We call on all Christians and citizens of good will to confront their own fears about homosexuality and to curb the humor and discrimination that offend homosexual persons. We understand that having a homosexual orientation brings with it enough anxiety, pain and issues related to self-acceptance without society bringing additional prejudicial treatment.

This is our universal call.

Application

In applying this teaching, three things make a difference:
Religious Formation. We must create awareness and educate all lay leaders, catechists, and ministers about this teaching and its application. Religious education programs should always

include this teaching in their curriculum along with reflection about real-life scenarios. Furthermore, pastors and parish staff need to reflect on how this teaching can openly be preached about at mass whenever appropriate (such as on the anniversary of the Orlando shooting or during Pride month), and how we can better educate parishioners and ministry leaders about this principle.

Awareness. Better education and awareness about the needs of the LGBTQ community, including issues of social justice and how this part of the Body of Christ is still a vulnerable group, would be helpful.

Learning from Lived Experience. Learning to be a listening Church to LGBTQ Catholics can educate us about their lived experience. We must learn and teach others to listen to a variety of stories of LGBTQ Catholics to understand the ways in which LGBTQ persons are still vulnerable in our society and in our church environments.

ALL ARE CALLED TO CHASTITY

Chastity means the integration of sexuality within the person.

Christ is the model of chastity. Every baptized person is called to lead a chaste life, each according to his particular state of life.

The chaste person maintains the integrity of the powers of life and love placed in him. This integrity. . .tolerates neither a double life nor a duplicity in speech.

Catechism of the Catholic Church, §§2394–95, 2338

Finally, the third piece of Church doctrine regards chastity. *Each baptized person,* (meaning *all* Catholics) is called to chastity. The beauty of the teaching on chastity is often misunderstood by lay leaders, not only regarding gay people but also themselves. The most common misunderstanding is the fact that many people often confuse chastity with celibacy. I often hear people say that "gays have to be celibate." This statement is wrong because the teaching that applies here concerns chastity not celibacy.

Why does this matter? First, the teachings of chastity and priestly celibacy are beautiful, but they are not the same and should not be conflated and reduced to less than what they are. Second, by conflating the two, the meaning of chastity is reduced to either mere abstinence or to a lack of a marital commitment. Chastity is deeper, more profound, and has a broader meaning.

The Practice of "Othering"

Before defining *chastity*, let me explain why understanding chastity is essential and necessary. "Othering" is the practice of viewing or treating a person or a group of people as different from the self and alien to oneself. When applied to Church doctrine, it involves seeing doctrine as applying only to the "other" and not to the self.

Saying that the teaching that applies to gay persons is "celibacy" is wrong (per the *Catechism*) and it effectively creates in the lay leaders' mind an illusion of "othering," a belief that they are exempt from whatever teaching gay persons are subject to. This othering makes it easier to point fingers and judge.

Per the *Catechism*, all persons—both heterosexual and homosexual—are called to a life of chastity. The same teaching applies to LGBTQ and heterosexual persons alike.

So, what is chastity? Let us first consider chastity broadly, and then, in the following section, we can discuss how it applies specifically to LGB persons.

SEXUAL ORIENTATION VS. GENDER IDENTITY

Sexual orientation can be defined as enduring emotional, romantic, and/or sexual attraction to other people. The labels "lesbian," "gay," "heterosexual," and "bisexual" are examples of such orientations. Gender identity and gender expression, however, can be defined as one's innermost concept of self as male, female, a blend of both, or neither—how individuals perceive themselves and how they present themselves to the world. The label "transgender" is related to gender identity, not to sexual orientation. "Being transgender does not imply any specific sexual orientation. Therefore, transgender people may identify as straight (heterosexual), or as gay, lesbian, bisexual, etc."[7] Transgender people are not always LGB; they can be, and often are, heterosexual. Whenever doctrine refers to a homosexual orientation, it refers to LGB persons (orientation), not to gender identity. This section is about chastity and is an analysis specific to sexual behavior and not about identity. The *Catechism of the Catholic Church* does not specifically mention the word "transgender" and does not yet have a section on gender identity, only on homosexuality and sexual behavior. Further learning on the differences between orientation and gender identity is encouraged.

---

7. "Sexual Orientation and Gender Identity Definition," Human Rights Campaign, accessed February 15, 2020, https://www.hrc.org.

What Is Chastity?

The *Catechism* defines *chastity* as "the integration of sexuality within the person" (§2395). Essentially, chastity is making sure that any sexual act that happens in our lives is integrated with our whole being—our emotions, our thoughts, our spirit, and our future. In other words, it is an integration of body and spirit (see §2332). Sexuality, which is a gift, concerns not only its physical aspects, but something much deeper. Among other things, it concerns affectivity, the capacity to love and to be loved, and the ability to form deep bonds of communion with others (see §2332). Church doctrine says that this integration of sexuality comes to its fullness under sacramental marriage (see §2360–61). However, each person must live chastity "according to his particular state of life" (see §2394).

To clarify and to highlight areas where people often get confused, here are some examples:

Example 1: We have a person, gay or straight, who is single and who meets someone one day and decides to have sex with that person the same day with the intent to never see each other again (commonly known as a one-night stand) and with zero interest for the well-being of that person. Is that person being chaste? The answer is no. The person, here, is not integrating the sexual act with their whole being, with their emotions, their thoughts, their spirit, nor their future. The sexual act in this case is more for biological relief and is not integrated with the whole being.

So, when we say that each person must practice chastity "according to his particular state of life," in the case of an individual who is single, that person would be encouraged to be "chaste in continence," or more simply, to be abstinent (§2349). This is also the type of chastity that is encouraged in teenagers.[8] Because teenagers are still forming their person-ality, getting to know themselves, and making plans for their future, practicing self-mastery in abstinence is advised.

In my experience, this type of scenario is the most com-mon scenario that comes to mind when lay leaders think of chastity. Even for those lay leaders who understand that chas-tity and celibacy are not the same, most laypersons still think that chastity means solely "abstinent while single." While in this scenario such a definition would be accurate, such a sim-plistic understanding of chastity robs the person of its true, deeper, broader, most valuable meaning.

Example 2: There is a man and a woman who are sacra-mentally married. They love each other, they are having sex because they are a couple, but they are integrating this sexual act with the love for each other, with their thoughts, and their future life together, and they are faithful to each other. Are they being chaste? The answer is yes. These people are being chaste even though they are having sex, because they are inte-grating the sexual act with their whole being. Chastity does not always mean abstinence, rather it must be applied "each according to his particular state of life." In the case of a married couple, they would be encouraged to live conjugal chastity, in other words, it is normal and healthy for a married couple to have sex and they would continue to be chaste provided they are integrating the sexual act with their whole being, with their thoughts, their feelings, and their future. Therefore, chastity is not just about abstinence or lack of sex, chastity is about inte-gration of the sexual act.[9]

---

8. "Self-mastery is a *long and exacting work.* One can never consider it acquired once and for all. It presupposes renewed effort at all stages of life. The effort required can be more intense in certain periods, such as when the personality is being formed during childhood and adolescence" (CCC 2342).

9. See "The acts in marriage by which the intimate and chaste union of the spouses takes place are noble and honorable; the truly human performance of these acts fosters the self-giving they signify and enriches the spouses in joy and gratitude"

In addition to the focus on integration, a common thread between these first two examples is the personal work of self-mastery and temperance. This common thread is essential to the understanding of chastity and its higher value.

Example 3: Consider the case of a man and a woman who are sacramentally married but are cheating on each other (or one of them is cheating). They are still having sex because they are a married couple, but for the one who is cheating, there is no integration of the sexual act with the emotions, the mind, and their future together. Are they being chaste? The answer is that the person who is cheating is not. Note that even though they are sacramentally married, they are not being chaste because the sexual act is not integrated. So, again, chastity is about integration. Just because someone is sacramentally married, it does not mean that the person is being chaste. Sacramental marriage does not always equal chastity.

Also note how the act of cheating triggers another aspect of the teaching of chastity: "The chaste person… tolerates neither a double life nor a duplicity." A double life, a life of lying, a life of hiding things, a life of being disloyal to the agreement made by the couple, is not an integrated life.

Example 4: Finally, consider a man and a woman who are sacramentally married. They love each other, they are having sex because they are a couple, and they are integrating this sexual act with the love for each other, with their thoughts, and their future together, and they are faithful to each other. However, they cannot bear children because one of them is sterile. Are they being chaste? The answer is yes. Just like the people in our first example, this couple is being chaste even though they are having sex, because they are integrating the sexual act with their whole being. When it comes to conjugal

---

and "Fidelity expresses constancy in keeping one's given word. God is faithful…. Through conjugal chastity, they bear witness to this mystery before the world," CCC 2362, 2365.

chastity, Church doctrine emphasizes procreation, fecundity, and being open to the transmission of life.[10] Yet the fact that a couple cannot naturally have children does not mean the couple is not integrating the sexual act with their whole being, with their feelings, their mind, their future, their spirit, and so on—that the couple is not being chaste. This is something that needs more reflection by the Church.

The Underlying Basis of Chastity

As someone who has been involved in young adult ministry for more than fifteen years and who has heard countless others teach about chastity, I am always sad whenever I hear someone teach chastity as a mere abstinence while single. In fact, we do our youth, our young adults, and our adults a disservice by teaching such a simplification of this term.

Chastity is not simply a rule for people to follow. It is grounded in the development of virtues, especially on the cardinal virtue of temperance.[11] Temperance, which is an invitation to self-mastery and to the development of our willpower and discipline, is the basis of chastity. Having the wisdom to give sexuality its due value regardless of our marital state and the strength to be true to agreements made with the person we commit to for a lifetime is fundamental. The discipline required is what makes one a disciple, not just the blind following of a rule one barely understands.

As religious educators, we must teach the cardinal virtues and their practical importance. These virtues and values can help guide our entire life, not just sexuality. The cardinal

10. "It is necessary that each and every marriage act remain ordered *per se* to the procreation of human life....Fecundity is a gift, an end of marriage, for conjugal love naturally tends to be fruitful," CCC 2366. See also §§2332, 2335, 2363, and 2366–79.

11. The four classic cardinal virtues in Christianity are temperance, prudence, courage (or fortitude), and justice. Christianity derives the three theological virtues of faith, hope, and love (charity) from 1 Cor 13. Together these make up the seven virtues.

virtues—coming from the Latin *cardo* meaning "hinge, chief point, or axis"—are at the core of making wise choices. Having the discipline and strength to make wise choices, to exercise our cardinal values, can result in spiritual improvement that goes beyond one single aspect of ourselves, beyond just sexuality. The development of virtues is required for one to practice an adult spirituality; otherwise, we risk becoming adults who have the spirituality of a child.

Application

Now that I have explained chastity in general, let us reflect as to what it means for LGB persons and how the teaching is often applied discriminatorily. As mentioned above, all baptized persons are called to a life of chastity that each person must live "according to his particular state of life." Chastity requires integration, and for those who are sexually active, Church doctrine informs us that such integration happens most fully within the context of sacramental marriage. Because sacramental marriage is only available between a man and a woman, current doctrine says that to be chaste, the gay person is not to marry and to remain abstinent—which is why the teaching is often confused with celibacy. As noted earlier, while the result for LGB people is similar to celibacy, there are some differences. First, the teaching of chastity applies to *all* persons, not just to LGBTQ people and to priests. Second, this teaching is often applied discriminatorily against LGBTQ persons. Finally, when Church doctrine is not followed, pastoral sensitivity exists toward heterosexual persons but not LGBTQ persons.

Discriminatory Application

My work in young adult ministry began after I joined a young adult group in my parish. To clarify, young adult ministries are for people between the ages of eighteen and thirty-five years old. A couple years after I joined, I became part of the group's leadership table and served as leader for three years. Many young adults who belonged to my youth group have been very successful in finding a husband or a wife among the members of the group and getting sacramentally married. I would like to believe that this success rate is due to our focus on virtues and a more mature approach to evangelization.

In my young adult group, the topic of chastity was, of course, part of our integral curriculum. However, whenever a girl and a guy from the group decided to start a relationship, the leadership team never assumed that the couple was having sex. Our reaction was always one of happiness and would approach the relationship with an attitude of respect for the privacy of the couple and trusting the heterosexual couple, assuming they will do their best.

The reaction to gay people, however, is not the same. A gay person is often judged harshly even if the person is single and not even in a relationship. The moment someone who is openly gay joins a ministry, ministry leaders and others often assume the person is sexually active—and many other assumptions and prejudices come with this assumption. This is evidenced by one of the statements I hear most often from lay leaders, and sometimes from the pulpit, when talking about LGBTQ persons: "We love the sinner but hate the sin."

Aren't we all sinners? Yet those who use this phrase are, consciously or unconsciously, assuming that the LGBTQ person is "sinning in a way that I don't sin." In other words, there is an assumption that the person is sexually active with a same-sex partner or a myriad of other assumptions such as that the person is a pedophile, promiscuous, unfaithful, addicted to sex, and so on.

Many Catholics don't give themselves the opportunity to get to know the person in front of them and allow for prejudices to cloud their vision of that person. LGBTQ persons are not even given the benefit of the doubt. Why would anyone want to remain in such a community? Why would anyone want to join a group where those who minister act more like the Pharisees than like Jesus?

There is also a disparity in applying the principles of the dignity of the human person and the principle against discrimination; these principles also apply to LGBTQ people.

Pastoral Sensitivity

Let's consider how the leadership team of my young adult group would respond if they discovered that the guy/girl couple from our group were indeed having sex before marriage. Even though we would be aware that they are failing to live a chaste life, we would still love them, we would still accept them, and we would still walk with them on their journey of faith. We would never say, "You're evil." "You're going to hell." "You're dragging others to hell." "You're possessed." "You can no longer attend the ministry." "You can never serve in ministry." There is an unspoken rule that makes room for pastoral sensitivity for heterosexual persons who fail to live up to the highest Catholic ideals—assuming they are doing the best they can and creating space for human error. Furthermore, we tend to see the entire person and to understand that, even if someone is failing to live up to one part of Church doctrine, the person can still be a good Christian.

Pastoral sensitivity is the most common response we see in ministry to heterosexual persons who fail to live a chaste life—having sex before marriage, masturbating, cheating, and divorcing, and remarrying. This is not to say that heterosexual persons are not often judged by the community based on their sexual behavior; they are often judged as well. However, in ministry, pastoral sensitivity is a common response.

For LGBTQ persons, the response is different. Often, the moment a gay person decides to have a partner or fails to live up to the same teaching in any way, the pastoral sensitivity vanishes. Pastoral sensitivity is only extended while the LGB person "follows Church doctrine," specifically as it refers to chastity. In other words, pastoral sensitivity is only extended to those LGB persons who are either abstinent or who claim to be abstinent. This lack of pastoral sensitivity is based on a generalized culture of assuming the worst about LGBTQ people, of judging the other more harshly than we judge ourselves, and of reducing the LGBTQ person to merely their orientation or identity.

Pastoral Sensitivity to Same-Sex Couples

This section is a personal commentary about pastoral sensitivity toward LGBTQ Catholics who are in a committed same-sex relationship. Its purpose is to understand and minister better to LGBTQ Catholics who have a partner.

Church doctrine currently informs us that sacramental marriage is available only between a man and a woman. There are many reasons to justify this doctrine that are beyond the scope of this book. However, central to the discussion is whether a person chooses their orientation or whether people are created by God that way. While scientific research has shed some light on sexual orientation, the science regarding whether orientation is determined by nature, nurture, or a combination of both is inconclusive or limited.[12] The findings of scientific research are also beyond the scope of this book, but everyone is encouraged to learn more about them, as scientific research is a tool God has given us to better understand creation.

Regardless of the research, one thing is true. To extend

---

12. Historically, scientific research has been mostly focused on studying men and not women. Most research has also been done based on western countries and not eastern. The research samples are small and limited. Furthermore, most research only includes people who already identify as nonheterosexual, omitting the many who are still in the closet, those who are very private about their sexuality, those who accept their orientation but have never acted on it, and those who are still questioning.

pastoral sensitivity to same-sex couples, we must understand that a person's orientation is experienced as a given. The United States Catholic Bishops have acknowledged this in their 1997 pastoral letter, "Always Our Children," where they humbly acknowledged that the orientation of an LGBTQ person is "experienced as a given, not as something freely chosen." If an LGBTQ person's orientation is a given—something one is born with—then the first thing we should understand is that the desire to have an everlasting romantic bond with another is experienced as naturally to an LGBTQ person as it is to a heterosexual person. Consequently, we should not assume ill intent or a choice of "evil over good" when it comes to same-sex relationships.

When you dialogue with LGBTQ people and listen to their stories, they will often tell you, "This is how I was born; this is how I was made; this is how God made me." People who are in a committed same-sex relationship are not going against God. In fact, they are honoring a life of chastity—integrating their sexuality with other aspects of themselves—with the person whom their conscience and their discernment process tells them God created them to love, the person God created them to relate to emotionally, spiritually, physically, mentally, and romantically.

They may not know God's purpose, but they do not choose to go against Church doctrine. They would certainly not choose to experience all the discrimination and to struggle with people's judgment. That is the real struggle of LGBTQ people—the judgment, the misunderstanding, the discrimination, the being discredited. In the past, our Catholic bishops in the United States have recognized that an LGB orientation is a given. The least we can do now is extend some pastoral sensitivity and pastoral care based on this understanding.

God is a God of mystery, including God's creation. Even with the advances in scientific research, there are many things in nature and the universe that remain unexplained. This should be humbling rather than frightening and should remind us of the expansiveness of God's love. As much as we would like to trap the entire universe in a box, God cannot be trapped in a box. As much as we would like to be like God and claim the infallible wisdom of one who has eaten the forbidden fruit, only God is all-knowing. God is still being revealed through creation, through the signs of the times, through love. Are we paying attention? Are we listening?

OTHER DOCTRINE AND LGBTQ CATHOLICS

Catholic doctrine applies to all Catholics including LGBTQ Catholics. This includes, but is not limited to, the primacy of the conscience and Catholic social teaching.

The Preferential Option for the Poor and Vulnerable

LGBTQ persons have been and continue to be a vulnerable group—a part of the Body of Christ that is hurting. While only 7 percent of all youth in America are classified as LGBTQ, as many as 40 percent of homeless youth belong to this group.[13] LGBTQ youth are 120 percent more likely to experience homelessness than non-LGBTQ youth.[14] This high level of homelessness is the result of family rejection, abuse, and poverty.[15] Once

---

13. "Our Issue," True Colors United, accessed February 10, 2021, https://truecolors united.org.

14. "Missed Opportunities: Youth Homelessness in America," Voices of Youth Count, accessed February 10, 2021, https://voicesofyouthcount.org.

15. "Our Issue," True Colors United, accessed February 10, 2021, https://truecolors united.org.

homeless, LGBTQ youth are also at an increased risk of being targeted by human traffickers.[16]

Family rejection is detrimental to the overall emotional, physical, and mental well-being of LGBTQ persons.[17] Even if an LGBTQ person does not experience homelessness or family rejection, they are still likely to experience discrimination in housing, education, employment, and health care, which impedes their long-term ability to "attain and maintain economic security."[18] At worst, LGBTQ persons are still targets of hate crimes and killings.[19] Our Church often fails to recognize the vulnerability of LGBTQ persons. The teaching of preferential option for the vulnerable reminds us that the vulnerable are at the center of the gospel and especially when any analysis about policy is being made.

Respect for Human Life

Closely linked to the principle of the dignity of human life is the principle of the respect for human life. All life is sacred from the moment of conception until natural death. Killings motivated by sexual orientation or gender identity are seldom accounted for and seldom prosecuted as a hate crime. Transgender people, in particular, suffer even more discrimination, violence, social and economic marginalization, and abuse, with transgender women of color being more likely to be murdered

---

16. "LGBTQ+ Youth at Increased Risk of Human Trafficking, New Survey Says," U.S. Catholic Sisters Against Human Trafficking, accessed February 10, 2021, https://sistersagainsttrafficking.org.

17. "Publications," Family Acceptance Project, accessed February 10, 2021, https://familyproject.sfsu.edu.

18. Caitlin Rooney and Charlie Whittington, "Protecting Basic Living Standards for LGBTQ People," Center for American Progress, accessed February 10, 2021, https://www.americanprogress.org.

19. "New FBI Hate Crimes Report Shows Increases in Anti-LGBTQ Attacks," HRC, accessed February 10, 2021, https://www.hrc.org.

in the United States and worldwide.[20] The Church should support policy efforts that can help determine the leading causes of violent death among the LGBTQ community. In addition to collecting data, the Church should support the use of government resources to prevent violence against transgender women and prioritize prosecutions against offenders.[21] Increased funding for antibias and hate crime investigation training is also essential.

Respect for human life, however, goes beyond the act of defending the right to be alive in support for a right to a dignified life, such as making sure people—especially the poor and vulnerable—have adequate access to health care, housing, and basic needs.

The Right to Work, the Common Good, and Solidarity with Workers

The Church recognizes work as a fundamental right.[22] This includes the right to a just wage, the right to rest, the right to a pension, the right to join a union, the right that one's personality in the workplace should be safeguarded "without suffering any affront to one's conscience or personal dignity," and more. Because of the moral implications that work has on social life, the Church considers unemployment a "real social disaster"[23] and an affront to the common good.

As noted earlier, the Church also recognizes that hatred, harassment, and discrimination of LGBTQ persons must not be

20. Rebecca L. Stotzer, "Data Sources Hinder Our Understanding of Transgender Murders," *American Journal of Public Health*, September 2017, https://www.ncbi.nlm.nih.gov/pmc/articles/PMC5551619/.

21. "100 Days Out: Trump v. Biden on LGBTQ Equality," HRC, accessed February 10, 2021, https://www.hrc.org.

22. *Compendium of the Social Doctrine of the Church*, §287, accessed February 10, 2021, http://www.vatican.va.

23. *Compendium of the Social Doctrine of the Church*, §287.

tolerated,[24] and the *Catechism* states that "every sign of unjust discrimination in their regard should be avoided" (§2358).

Based on these two principles, Catholics should encourage their governments to pass comprehensive nondiscrimination protections for LGBTQ people in employment, housing, credit, health care, and education. While religious institutions have the right to ask for religious exemptions to laws that run afoul of their beliefs, we must be careful not to invalidate LGBTQ-positive policies in their entirety, otherwise, we risk running afoul of our own doctrine.

Furthermore, even when using religious exemptions, we must discern the way the exemption is used to avoid discrimination that is unjust and unethical. The firings of LGBTQ persons who work in Catholic schools and institutions is currently one of the most problematic issues in the United States and the world.[25] While we recognize that Catholic schools exist to provide a Catholic education and to further Catholic values, teachers are usually not zealously policed to make sure they comply with every aspect of Church doctrine, unless they are an LGBTQ person. No other part of Church teaching is enforced as zealously as teachings of marriage and anti-LGBTQ rhetoric, and no other group of people is affected as often by this enforcement as LGBTQ people. While caring for the poor, the migrant, and the vulnerable is at the heart of the gospel, virtually no one is fired for failing to comply with these and other core teachings.

Finally, we must be careful not to use scare tactics to gain religious exemptions. Vulnerable groups are often pitted against each other: gay people against children; transgender

---

24. Fr. Chris Ponnet and Arthur Fitzmaurice, "Illuminating Church Teachings on Homosexuality—REC Handout," LGBTCatholics.org, accessed on January 21, 2021, https://lgbtcatholics.files.wordpress.com/2019/03/illuminating-church-teachings-on-homosexuality-recongress2014-handout-3-04.pdf.

25. "List of LGBTQ-Related Church Employment Disputes," New Ways Ministry, accessed February 17, 2021, https://www.newwaysministry.org.

people against women. A rhetoric that paints gay people as pedophiles and transgender people as opportunistic to gain religious exemptions must be avoided.

LGBTQ people are a vulnerable group, but we often fail to recognize the vulnerability because we have failed to walk beside them, and we have failed to listen to their life experiences as Jesus would.

SCRIPTURE

First, what is the Bible? The *Catechism* defines the Bible as a collection of books written by men but inspired by the Holy Spirit (§105). Catholicism is not a fundamentalist religion, Catholicism is not a "religion of the book."[26] Fundamentalist religions read the Bible literally, where all that matters is that which is written.

Catholics are called to read the Bible through what is termed a historical-critical method. Consequently, in reading the Bible we must ask ourselves such things as the following: "Who wrote this particular book?" "Who is the author?" "Who is the author's intended 'audience'?" "What is the author's historical and cultural context?" "What type of book, or literary genre, is it? Is it a historical book or a theological story?" "What is the historical and cultural context of the book as a whole?"[27] This

26. "Still, the Christian faith is not a 'religion of the book.' Christianity is the religion of the 'Word' of God, 'not a written and mute word, but incarnate and living.' If the Scriptures are not to remain a dead letter, Christ, the eternal Word of the living God, must, through the Holy Spirit, 'open (our) minds to understand the Scriptures'" (CCC 108).

27. "In Sacred Scripture, God speaks to man in a human way. To interpret Scripture correctly, the reader must be attentive to what the human authors truly wanted to affirm, and to what God wanted to reveal to us by their words. In order to discover the sacred authors' intention, the reader must take into account the conditions of their time and culture, the literary genres in use at that time, and the modes of

method gives the reader greater context in reading what is written in the Bible.

Our reading of the Bible must be responsible and focus less on the mere memorization of isolated biblical verses taken out of context and more on an understanding of "the content and unity of the whole Scripture" (§112), always remembering that the Gospels are the heart of all the Scriptures because they are the principal source for the life and teaching of Jesus (§125).[28]

Many biblical scholars have done groundbreaking work analyzing the biblical passages that are most often referred to when speaking about homosexual persons. The focus of this book is not to explain each one of those passages because, first, there are plenty of Scripture scholars who can do a much better job, and second, this is a task that the Magisterium needs to undertake more deeply and more fully in the future (see §85). However, to illustrate the importance of the historical-critical method in reading the Bible, let's consider the story of Sodom and Gomorrah, perhaps the most familiar one used against LGBTQ people.

Sodom and Gomorrah (Gen 19:1–11)

This is a story that people often quote as being about "God destroying a city because of homosexuality."

The story is about God who is about to destroy the cities of Sodom and Gomorrah because of their inhabitants' wickedness. God then sends two angels. The two angels, in the form

---

feeling, speaking and narrating then current....For the fact is that truth is differently presented and expressed in the various types of historical writing, in prophetical and poetical texts, and in other forms of literary expression." "But since Sacred Scripture is inspired, there is another and no less important principle of correct interpretation, without which Scripture would remain a dead letter....Sacred Scripture must be read and interpreted in the light of the same Spirit by whom it was written" (CCC 109, 111).

28. See also CCC 127: "There is no doctrine which could be better, more precious and more splendid than the text of the Gospel."

of men, enter the city, and Lot greets them and invites them to stay in his house. Lot's gesture is a gesture of hospitality to the foreigner. The angels end up accepting Lot's invitation and spend the night at his house. It is at this point that all of the men who inhabit the city come to Lot's house; they knock on the door and demand that Lot bring the two men outside because they want to "know them."

It is important to understand that in some biblical passages, the cultural meaning of "know" is different from what we would understand today. In the Bible, to "know" someone can sometimes mean "to have sex with."[29] According to theologians and biblical scholars, the story of Sodom and Gomorrah is one of those passages where "know" means "to have sex with."

Also note the consensual versus nonconsensual nature of these encounters. For example, if a biblical passage were to use the word *know* according to this cultural meaning and it said, "I want to 'know' your daughter," then this wouldn't mean the person wants to "meet" the daughter; rather it would mean "I want to have sex with your daughter." Because the sex is nonconsensual and is forced on the person, the intended meaning would be "I want to rape your daughter."

In the story of Lot, Scripture tells us that *all* the men in the city came to Lot's door and told him to bring the foreigners outside because they wanted to "know" them. This is not a story about two people who love each other, and this is most definitely not a story about two people who are consensually entering into any kind of relationship. This story is not even about a random, consensual, sexual encounter, no. This is a story about attempted rape, gang rape to be exact. Furthermore, because all of the men in the city came to Lot's door, it is very likely most of them were heterosexual, not homosexual. This story is about something as wicked and as horrible as

29. Herbert Haag, A. van den Born, and S. de Ausejo, *Diccionario de la Biblia* (Barcelona: Herder Editorial, 1963).

attempted gang rape. Why in the world would heterosexual men want to rape other men for no reason? Gang rape was a well-recognized practice of biblical times that was used against enemies and against the vulnerable as a way to humiliate them and show them who is "in charge."

The story of Sodom and Gomorrah is about showing these two foreigners "who is the boss." In fact, this story is about the lack of hospitality to the foreigner, the arrogance and lack of concern for the poor and needy, and the abuse that foreigners, including Lot himself, suffered. That was the wickedness in these people's hearts and that level of wickedness was the reason why Sodom and Gomorrah were destroyed.

Other Scripture Passages

Biblical scholars have done significant work analyzing the biblical passages that mention the word *homosexual* or that are most often used to ostracize homosexual persons. Daniel A. Helminiak, PhD, a respected theologian and Roman Catholic priest, drawing from the work of the foremost scholars on the subject, explains many of these passages in his book *What the Bible Really Says about Homosexuality*. In the past, much of this work has historically been ignored, criticized, or simply not supported. However, in recent years there has been an increase in interest for the formal study of these and other texts.

The first thing we must be aware of is the fact that the word *homosexual* per se did not exist in biblical times. The word *homosexual* was coined in the late nineteenth century[30] and was first used in translations of the Bible in 1946.[31] To truly understand the meaning of each of the passages where

30. Brent Pickett, "Homosexuality," *Stanford Encyclopedia of Philosophy*, Stanford University, accessed on February 10, 2021, https://plato.stanford.edu/entries/homosexuality/.

31. Daniel A. Helminiak, *What the Bible Really Says about Homosexuality* (New Mexico: Alamo Square Press, 2000).

the word *homosexual* now appears, we must study the words used in the original texts—the words in Hebrew, Aramaic, and Greek.

When the word *homosexuality* first came into existence in the late nineteenth century, it was used to refer to all activity that involved people of the same sex, even if it was nonconsensual. The passages that now have the word *homosexuality* in them originally referred to scenarios of sexual violence against a person of the same sex, acts such as rape, pedophilia/pederasty, forced prostitution, and pagan rituals. The biblical passages do not speak of same-sex relationships of love and mutuality, nor do they speak of a state-approved lifelong commitment to a same-sex partner, because that was not even an option at the time the biblical books were written.

The most recent and significant development in biblical interpretation for Catholics comes from the Pontifical Biblical Commission. Toward the end of 2019, the Vatican's Pontifical Biblical Commission published a new book on the anthropological vision of Scripture titled *What Is Man? An Itinerary of Biblical Anthropology.*[32] This is a lengthy study of biblical anthropology that explores topics such as creation, sexuality, marriage, and ecology, to mention a few. The study is an authoritative reflection on certain biblical subjects over which theologians often clash with each other and "offers theologians and catechists observations of modern society's views on man today and contrasts them with Scripture."

When addressing the biblical account of Sodom, for instance, the Pontifical Biblical Commission states,

---

32. Pontificia Commissione Biblica, *"Che Cosa E L'uomo: Un Itinerario di Antrologia Bíblica,"* Libreria Editrice Vaticana, 2019. The online version may be found here: https://www.vatican.va/roman_curia/congregations/cfaith/pcb_documents/rc_con_cfaith_doc_20190930_cosa-e-luomo_it.pdf.

[This text] is not intended to present the image of an entire city dominated by irrepressible homosexual cravings; rather, it denounces the conduct of a social and political entity that does not want to welcome the foreigner with respect, and therefore claims to humiliate him, forcing him to undergo an infamous treatment of submission.[33]

Regarding the story of Sodom and Gomorrah, the Pontifical Biblical Commission concluded,

[It] illustrates a sin that consists in the lack of hospitality, with hostility and violence towards the stranger, a behavior judged very serious and therefore deserving to be sanctioned with the utmost severity, because the rejection of the different, of the needy and defenseless stranger, is a principle of social disintegration, having in itself a deadly violence that deserves an adequate punishment.[34]

Clearly, responsible biblical scholarship about homosexuality is rare and greatly needed. We also need to question what we have heard in the past about this subject, what we have heard or read in certain Catholic media, and even our own preconceived ideas. We should not be afraid to get close to the margins and to improve our biblical formation. I encourage all laypersons and ministers to take biblical formation and religion courses at a community college or university. Catholic universities, partnered with dioceses or on their own, often have formation or leadership programs that do not require formal enrollment.

If you are an LGBTQ Catholic who has been hurt by authority figures or by people who have used Scripture as a weapon

33. https://www.newwaysministry.org.
34. https://www.newwaysministry.org.

against you, know that God hurts with you. You are part of the Body of Christ and God loves you. Do not be afraid to learn more about the Scriptures. Allow yourself to learn about Jesus and to be close to God. Allow yourself to feel and to know that you are a beloved child of God.

THE *CATECHISM OF THE CATHOLIC CHURCH*

Throughout this chapter, we have already referred to significant quotes from the *Catechism* regarding homosexuality. However, when most people use the *Catechism* regarding this topic, they often focus on a specific phrase: "intrinsically disordered." What does "intrinsically disordered" mean? How much should we concern ourselves with this phrase?

I was first introduced to the term "intrinsically disordered" during one of my weekly meetings at the youth group I was involved in, when I was sixteen years old. A lay preacher had been invited to give us a talk about homosexuality and, by the end of the talk, I felt a deep shame that had nothing to do with who I was or who I am, but rather with how the preacher defined me: an intrinsically disordered and evil person. As I grew in leadership, in my faith, and in my own religious formation, I came to understand that many of the lay and ordained preachers who use this term lack a deeper understanding of doctrine and pastoral sensitivity.

First, the *Catechism* was not written by or for the average layperson. The *Catechism* was written by people who have a background in theology and philosophy. While it was intended to be a guide for all, it is better understood by those who understand the theological and philosophical terms within it. For instance, for the average person, the term "intrinsically disordered" might summon references to "mental disorder" or "disease."

Essentially, the term "intrinsically disordered" in the *Catechism* refers primarily to an act, not a person. The term is directly linked to "chastity" and the importance of integrating every sexual act with the whole being according to each person's particular state of life, as noted above. Consequently, an adequate understanding of chastity must precede an adequate understanding of "intrinsically disordered," and a pastoral approach to chastity must precede any responsible use of this term.

Second, in the *Catechism* many acts are referred to as "sins gravely contrary to chastity" or "intrinsically disordered." For example, masturbation is "intrinsically [and gravely] disordered" (§2352). While masturbation is very common, the term "intrinsically disordered" is almost always used against gay people and not against the many who masturbate—gay, straight, men, women, lay, and ordained.

The term "intrinsically disordered" is often used irresponsibly, and maybe through ignorance, we don't realize that the term applies to many other scenarios, including those who wield it as a sword against gay people. We must stop using the terms in the *Catechism* as bullets or swords. That is not the purpose for which they were intended.

5

PASTORAL CARE

From 2015 through 2016, Pope Francis called for an Extraordinary Jubilee of Mercy. According to the USCCB, "Pope Francis called this particular Extraordinary Jubilee of Mercy to direct our attention and actions 'on mercy so that we may become a more effective sign of the Father's actions in our lives...a time when the witness of believers might grow stronger and more effective.'" In other words, this was a time to discern mercy, to observe ourselves, and to figure out ways to practice mercy. Many of us who actively and consciously participated in the Jubilee of Mercy lived the year as a time of grace.

When we think of mercy, we often think of "compassion" or "forgiveness" toward someone who has hurt us or done us wrong; someone whom we might punish but rather choose to be merciful because this brings us spiritual gain. The problem with this understanding of mercy is that we put ourselves above everyone else: "because I am merciful, I forgive you"; "because I am a good person, I will be compassionate." Here, we place our ego before mercy; we are merciful because of the spiritual good it brings us. Furthermore, it is a missed opportunity to get deeply in touch with the source of mercy, which is detached love—Jesus's love.

The etymological definition of the word *mercy* in Spanish is *misericordia*, which comes from two Latin words, *miserere*, which means "misery" or "pain," and *cor*, which means "heart."

Therefore, *misericordia* means "feeling the other person's pain in your own heart." It is from this pain, of feeling it in your own heart, that you are compassionate, not because you are better, but because you feel that person's pain and you respond to the pain with love.

So, how can we feel the pain of someone we don't know? How can we feel the pain of "the other"? How can we feel the pain of someone with whom we disagree? How can we feel the pain of someone whom we would rather not have to encounter?

Pope Francis suggests three pastoral approaches that are useful to practice. These approaches, which we summarized in the previous chapter, involve becoming a Church of encounter, a listening Church, and a Church of accompaniment. It is through these pastoral approaches that we find the tools necessary for living mercifully and becoming a more pastoral Church.

A CHURCH OF ENCOUNTER

In his address to the lay movements on the vigil of Pentecost in 2013, Pope Francis exhorted us all to go to the margins:

> The Church must step outside herself. To go where? To the outskirts of existence, whatever they may be, but she must step out. Jesus tells us, "Go into all the world! Go! Bear witness to the Gospel!" But, what happens if we step out of ourselves? The same that can happen to anyone who comes out of the house and onto the street: an accident. But I tell you, I far prefer a church that has had a few accidents to a Church that has fallen sick from being closed. Go out, go out!

There are many Catholics, not just LGBTQ Catholics, who live on the margins of society. Some have been explicitly excluded from the Church for failing to fulfill many tenets of doctrine—for example, those divorced and remarried, those who have had sex before marriage, those who are cohabitating but not sacramentally married. These and others have decided to leave the Church. Many who live on the margins are vulnerable, yet many have a strong faith. Jesus is present at the margins of our society, but as Catholics we can often enclose ourselves in our zone of comfort and minister with and to the people and the groups with whom we feel comfortable. Jesus calls us to be with him and to be more like him.

Being a Church of encounter requires that we encounter people exactly where they are, not where we want them to be; it requires that we encounter people exactly as they are and without an agenda. Being a Church of encounter requires that we be open to friendship with people as they are, because a culture of encounter is a culture of friendship. If we are unable to enter into disinterested friendship with those who are different from us, we are refusing to see Jesus in them, and we are failing to be more like Jesus, because Jesus's model of encounter was based precisely on friendship: sharing a meal with strangers, inviting himself to their house, and listening to people's stories. As Pope Francis said in that same address to lay movements,

> With our Faith, we must create a culture of encounter, a culture of friendship, a culture in which we find brothers and sisters, in which we can also speak with those who think differently, as well as others who hold other beliefs....They all have something in common with us: they are images of God; they are all children of God.

Encountering people exactly as they are means serving each other, loving each other, and becoming each other's friend exactly as they are. We shouldn't wait for the other to be perfect, for the other to be how we think they should be, for the other to do what we think they should do. It is about encountering others exactly where they are, in whatever part of the journey they are in. That is where true encounter happens.

A LISTENING CHURCH

Encounter is not about physical bodies being in the same space at the same time. Rather, encounter requires a connection of friendship with those who are different. For true encounter to exist, we must learn to be a listening Church.

The art of listening requires a detachment from our self-interest. Have you ever caught yourself "listening" to someone while you are already thinking about the next thing you will say to the person? This thought may be a story that you believe is similar or you may want to give the person your advice, to tell them what to do, or to emit judgment. In all these scenarios, it is our self-interest to have the attention turned to us, to feel useful, to feel we are helping or furthering a certain cause, or to end the conversation quickly because we need to run to our next commitment.

It is extremely hard to sit still without thinking of our next participation in the conversation and simply listen. It is hard to listen to those we love, and much harder to listen to those with whom we disagree or those who are different from us. Yet we will not reach encounter and friendship with those who are different from us if we don't master the art of listening. Our overlapping thoughts cloud our vision and can prevent us from listening to, learning from, and seeing the person before us.

Being a listening Church means listening to learn from the other person's lived experience. Whenever we are learning about something for the first time, asking questions can be helpful: "How did that make you feel?" or "What happened next?" Remember that we are all human beings, that we are all still learning. Remember that each person's life and circumstances are different. Remember that God's grace is something that we can receive through others, and who better than the people whom we usually don't understand. If we can become this listening Church, we will be able to develop a fraternal love for those we listen to, as we learn about their pains, their glory, their faith, and their lived experience.

Fr. Greg Boyle, who started Homeboy Industries in East Los Angeles and ministers to those on the margins, once said,

> In my thirty years of ministry to gang members in Los Angeles, the most significant reversal of course for me happened somewhere during my sixth year. I had mistakenly tried to "save" young men and women trapped in gang life. But then, in an instant... I discovered that you do not go to the margins to rescue anyone. But if we go to the margins, everyone finds rescue.

A CHURCH OF ACCOMPANIMENT

Once we have encountered someone on the margins of society and have learned to listen, we are ready to accompany each other on our journeys of faith. The concept of accompaniment is like being blood related, or family. We do not choose our family. We may often disagree with our family members, yet we do our best to walk together on this journey of life. No one's family is perfect. Some families are more functional than others; others are extremely dysfunctional.

Our Church family is not perfect either, but God is perfect; Jesus is perfect; love is perfect. As St. Paul reminds us, love never fails, and because the greatest commandment is love (see 1 Cor 13:1–13), we must accompany each other on our journeys of faith, regardless of what those journeys look like.

6

YOUR JOURNEY OF DISCERNMENT

This book was never intended to be a means to an end, but more a beginning. Regardless of what part of the journey you are on, you have homework—to begin a journey of discernment. Your discernment begins with listening to (or reading) stories of LGBTQ Catholics and, if you are an LGBTQ Catholic, listening to stories of LGBTQ people whose story is different from yours. Because many readers may not know an LGBTQ Catholic, I will briefly share my own story in the hope that it will be the first of many other stories that you will listen to through your journey of discernment. First, however, I would like to provide some helpful suggestions as you listen to the lived experiences of LGBTQ persons.

First, you may hear a variety of stories. Not all stories of LGBTQ persons, however, are the same. Having heard the story of one or two persons in the LGBTQ community does not mean that you will know all there is about the lived experiences of an LGBTQ person.

Second, you will notice that sexual orientation is not just about sexuality. In fact, sexuality often occupies the back burner in most of the stories you will hear. Orientation relates to a person's emotional, physical, spiritual, and romantic connection and is often experienced in a nonsexual way, such as having an innocent crush on someone. This focus on a deep romantic emotional connection, rather than on sex, will be a constant theme throughout. Listen and don't discard such claims.

Third, as you hear different stories, you will notice some common themes: stories of deep faith and love, family rejection, self-doubt, denial, and acceptance. Many stories might reveal very painful journeys and, the more a person is in the margins, the more painful the story might be.

As noted earlier, many LGBTQ youth who are rejected by their families end up homeless and are often targets of human traffickers, who force them into prostitution. Even if an LGBTQ person is never homeless, when rejected by family, he or she may face other risks. The family acceptance project, a study by San Francisco State University, found that family rejection correlates directly with higher incidents of attempted suicide, depression, drug and substance abuse, and risky sexual behaviors. LGBTQ people who experience family rejection are more than eight times as likely to have attempted suicide, nearly six times as likely to report high levels of depression, more than three times as likely to use illegal drugs, and more than three times as likely to be at risk of contracting HIV/AIDS and/or other sexually transmitted diseases than those LGBTQ people who experience little or no family rejection. Family rejection, not the orientation, is the cause of such suffering.

Stories that include any of the difficult challenges mentioned above must be listened to with sensitivity and empathy. However, these experiences themselves should not be equated with being LGBTQ, nor should they be lumped together to refer to the "homosexual lifestyle." Having been able to escape human trafficking networks or overcome any of the above challenges should not be equated with being an ex-gay, as is often the case.

Fourth, as you listen to stories, you will also hear stories from bisexual people—people who are in what is called the continuum of sexual orientation. Unlike heterosexual persons who are wired to have an emotional, physical, spiritual, romantic connection with persons of the opposite sex, and unlike homosexual persons, who are wired to have an emotional, physical, spiritual, romantic connection with persons of the same sex, bisexual persons can develop such connections with either sex—at varying degrees.

This does not mean that bisexual persons are promiscuous, confused, or any other stereotype. Furthermore, a bisexual person can have feelings for someone of the same sex when they are young and years later have feelings for someone of the opposite sex, or vice versa. This does not mean they are choosing to be attracted to only one sex or that they have changed their orientation. Rather, it means their orientation allows for them to have this emotional connection with either sex and at varying times and degrees.

Finally, as you hear a variety of stories of LGBTQ persons, you will discover that, despite the differences, those persons are equally holy. You might listen to the story of someone who has chosen to remain single and abstinent; you might also listen to the story of someone who has a lifelong partner. At some point, you will see that those persons are equally holy. When you see this for the first time, it will be mind-blowing and you may not be able to understand it. Sit with this new realization and discern God's calling for you.

Before you start your journey of discernment, let me share part of my own story.

MY STORY

I've always known that I was different; ever since my very first memories I somehow knew this. When I was a little kid, I didn't really think about the difference, I just knew that I was.

When I was eleven years old, I realized that I liked someone—that I had a crush on a girl. Just like most people at some point in their lives have a crush on someone for the first time and out of nowhere, that's exactly what happened to me. It was as natural as any crush any heterosexual kid might have. I had never "experimented" or been sexually active. In fact, I was a nerdy kid not yet interested in all that stuff; it was an innocent crush. As innocent as it was, I never told anyone; I kept it to myself.

It was not until the age of seventeen that this feeling emerged again. As I was minding my own business in high school and doing my best to get good grades, I met the most wonderful girl I had ever met. Unlike my earlier crush, this time the feeling was mutual. Again, it was also an innocent crush—one of the purest feelings I had ever felt. The crush eventually gave birth to an innocent, loving relationship. This time I wanted to be able to share my feelings with those I cared about the most—my family.

My mom had always raised us with strong values and good virtues. She raised us to be disciplined, hard-working, loving, and honest. She was very nurturing and instilled in us a rich spiritual life. I wanted to be honest with my mom and to have better communication with her. My communication with my mom up to that point was not great, and I knew it had a lot to do with the fact that I was keeping this important part of myself to myself. Therefore, I decided to come out to her... for the first time. Mom listened to me, but she didn't know how to react to my confession.

As I mentioned in the first chapter, it is often said that when a child comes out of the closet, the parents go into the closet—they often have difficulty addressing the topic and decide not to address it at all. My mom listened to my confession, but she had many questions that she needed to process.

Like any good parent, she tried to do what she thought was best. One day after Mass someone gave her a flyer of an upcoming spiritual retreat for young adults. The "jóvenes group" of the parish—a young adult ministry in Spanish—was the organizer of this initiation retreat. My mom loved the idea and sent me to the retreat, perhaps hoping they would "cure me" of whatever it was that was going on with me. I didn't think I would like the retreat because, up until that point, my experience of Catholicism had been very negative. When I was growing up, some of my extended family had repeatedly used Catholicism to control, manipulate, and judge others. My mom's experience of Catholicism had also been very negative, but she was trying to hold on to whatever hope she could.

The retreat broke all my predictions and was the most wonderful experience! The jóvenes group that planned the retreat really focused on the message of the gospel and the person of Jesus. For the first time in my life, I had a personal and deep encounter with Jesus. I learned things about Jesus, about God, that I had never heard before, and the learning was also reflected in action. To be clear, this retreat was about more than just words. The young adults, who directed the retreat, were so loving, welcoming, selfless, and Jesus-like. For the first time, I experienced true Christian community and had found a treasure. I found a deep love within myself, I found Jesus, friendship, community, and I did not want to lose that treasure.

As loving as the group members were—and as much as I loved them—and many of them are now my close friends—I've often secretly wondered if the jóvenes would have approached me with the same love and trust had it been visibly apparent that I was gay. I knew some of the speakers who were invited to the retreat were antigay, so I always wondered if I would have been treated differently if I had been openly gay.

As time passed, the relationship with my girlfriend didn't work out and we broke up. I always thank God for the opportunity to know one of the purest feelings one can feel with someone who respected me and cared for me, even if we were not meant to be together for a lifetime.

Because I did not want to lose the treasure I had just found, I decided to take some time after my breakup and get to know myself better, to deepen my relationship with God, to learn what the Church, science, and other religions say about homosexuality, and to discern my own vocation. I wanted to take the time and space to discern all the questions I had and to discern what God wanted from me, but I knew most ministries did not offer a space for discernment for people who are openly gay—we are usually told what to do with our lives without creating a space for personal discernment and growth. Because I wanted to discern in peace, I decided to go back into the closet. This closeted period lasted for nearly ten years.

During that time, I focused on school, ministry, and was able to get a job and become independent. I became a youth leader at my youth group and was part of the leadership table for three years. I took several basic and advanced archdiocesan formation courses, and eventually became part of the Archdiocesan Pastoral Juvenil (young adult ministry) leadership team. As part of this team, I was a coordinator of formation courses for young adults and was even a radio host for five years on Catholic Radio in Los Angeles. I've been involved in young adult ministry for more than fifteen years, and I regularly teach formation courses for youth focused on social justice and Catholic social teaching. I've also been a lector and, yes, I also had my years in choir where I learned to play guitar; that is perhaps the gayest thing about me. I'm currently a eucharistic minister and continue to be a lector. During that same period, I also became a faith-based community organizer, putting my faith in action on issues such as mass incarceration, economic disparity, immigration, criminal justice, and more; working for a world where the human dignity of all is recognized, respected, and reflected in society.

Because I was completely focused on my personal growth and did not have any romantic interests, I thought that maybe the "pray the gay away approach" had worked. Toward the end of that ten-year period, I even decided to have a boyfriend.

I met a very handsome guy in church. Not only was he handsome, but he also had a kind heart. I thought that if I tried hard enough and prayed hard enough, life would be easier being heterosexual. We would have our "perfect" family pictures, and I would not have to face anyone's prejudices again. I later discovered that that is not how God works.

After being in a relationship with this boy for nearly two years, we started talking about our future and the possibility of marriage. I thought things were good and that marriage might be on the horizon; everything was going according to plan. Many Catholic sources I had consulted always emphasized how feelings are not important and the only thing that matters is the commitment. I was committed and disciplined, I felt that I could totally do this. Then I realized that God had different plans for me.

She came into my life. We were not meant to be, but she did remind me of who I am. "Oh God, I am still gay! I've always been gay!" I thought to myself ten years after my first coming out. I learned that feelings do matter, that feelings are the most natural thing, and that denying them or trying to bury them did not do anyone any good, especially myself. I also learned that feelings alone are not enough, a good balance of feelings and mature commitment must exist.

I realized that if I ever married the guy with whom I was in a relationship, I would be preventing him—and myself—from having the kind of mutual emotional, physical, spiritual, romantic connection that one is supposed to have with a spouse. I could not, in good conscience, do that to him nor to myself. I knew that if I did, it would be for selfish motives and that I would be using him; I would be marrying him out of fear, not out of love. I also realized this type of marriage would be the opposite of being chaste because, in being with him, I would not be integrating my sexuality with my whole being. I loved him like I love a brother, a friend, but that connection was not remotely spouse-like.

If I had married him, I would likely be living a life of duplicity because—unlike heterosexual folks who are wired to have a spouse-like connection with someone of the opposite sex and unlike bisexual folks who can have that type of connection with either sex—I am not wired that way. Coming out a second time was even more difficult than the first because now I had much more to lose, my entire world was built around my Catholicism and Jesus.

I knew my feelings were as natural as those of a heterosexual person, but for some reason, God made me different, and God must have a purpose for that difference. As scared as I was to tell people that I was gay, the scarier realization came when it dawned on me that my God-given vocation is to be with one person in a loving, committed lifelong relationship. Even though that person has not yet come into my life, I know that one day she will. "What will happen when we meet and formalize our relationship?" An overwhelming sadness and fear overtook me. "I will surely lose my treasure." I've felt God's embrace, letting me know that he loves me, that he formed my innermost being and knit me in my mother's womb. I've felt God's voice in the depths of my conscience, calling me to be truthful and not to be afraid.

During my second coming out, I felt this deep calling to start ministering to and with LGBTQ Catholics, such as myself. It was extremely difficult at the beginning but, thank God, I was not alone. I had met Martha and her husband, Javier Plascencia, during my time working in young adult ministry, and I knew about the ministry for parents of gay and lesbian persons they hosted. So I decided to go to one of their monthly meetings.

At the meeting, in tears, I told everyone present that I didn't know if there would ever be a place for me in the Church once I came out again and started publicly ministering to LGBTQ persons. I didn't know whether I should leave or stay.

This time was a sad, depressing, and dark moment in my life; trying to determine whether I should stay or leave the Church. It took months of discernment, during which time the parent group probably saw me cry more than I had in a long time. They always responded with love and words of hope. They helped me through this process, and I am forever grateful to them for that. They helped me remember that God loves me unconditionally, and it is thanks to them that I am still here, that I am still ministering.

Once I centered myself again in God's love, I had a conversation with my mom—ten years after that first conversation. This time, it was the best conversation we had ever had with each other. The conversation went for about five hours. She just listened to me for about two hours—just listened and asked questions to which I responded respectfully. Then I listened to her and her concerns for about two hours—just listened and asked questions, to which she respectfully and lovingly responded. My second coming out happened in a spirit of love, mutual respect, and sensitivity. It was a moment of healing, deep healing in my relationship with my mom.

It is now my entire hope and wish that one day every LGBTQ Catholic may experience these moments of healing with family. That is why I minister, because I know that the stories of LGBTQ Catholics often include, in varying degrees, a story of family separation, rejection, or misunderstanding. LGBTQ Catholics struggle. We struggle with the separation and disintegration of our families; we struggle with societal rejection and the effects of that rejection; and we struggle with self-love and with reconciling what we hear about God with God's love for us. Our families struggle reconciling their faith with their call to love their children. We also struggle with having to deal with all the prejudices of people who do not see the person in front of them, in our integrity, in our full dignity, in our love—the way God sees us.

Experiencing moments of healing and doing LGBTQ ministry has been the best thing that has ever happened to me. I've felt God's fingernail painfully scratching my heart and telling me, "Feed my people; help my people." In a world where people are hungry for love, feeding them a penal code is condemning them to starvation. God continues calling me to minister and to continue bringing him to the margins. I love doing LGBTQ ministry and helping others discern the difficult questions our Church is called to discern at this point.

Ninety-nine percent of the response to my ministry is usually positive. After every workshop, both parents and LGBTQ Catholics thank me, most often in tears, living small moments of healing. Others who are not parents or LGBTQ Catholics themselves also respectfully approach me to ask all kinds of questions about ministry. For the most part, the response is very positive, and yes, not everyone is fully accepting, but most people at least try to listen and discern.

Sometimes my heart also hurts with a deep pain when that 1 percent speaks. It never fails. There is always someone who is not there in a spirit of respect, compassion, and sensitivity; or even worse, someone who is outright hateful. It surprises me, because I am 100 percent certain that if I had met those people who criticize my work when I was involved in young adult ministry, they would have praised my work. I am still the same person; nothing has changed. If anything, I've improved. Yet, when I speak to those folks, my work is demonized, and I am demonized as well for absolutely no reason, demonized in God's name; "You shall not use the name of God in vain." I often think about all the amazing LGBTQ Catholics who grew up being model Catholics, but who left the Church after having been demonized in the name of Catholicism or, even worse, in the name of Jesus, in God's name. I often think about those who have been outright excluded from a ministry for being LGBTQ. I think about those who condemn us, but the math never adds up. I am not perfect, but I am most certainly not a bad person. More often than I'd like to admit, I question whether I should continue in the Church. I question it every day.

I am not the only one doing LGBTQ ministry. As highlighted throughout this book, there are hundreds of Catholics, including parents, LGBTQ Catholics themselves, ally priests, religious brothers and sisters, and so on, who are ministering at the parish, diocesan, national, or international level in different countries. However, compared to the overall Church and the magnitude of the need, there is still very few of us doing this ministry.

That is what I hope we can do together. I hope that we can discern how to create spaces of community for all LGBTQ Catholics, starting in your parish. I know that one day every parish will have a space, a community of love, of true respect, compassion, and sensitivity, where LGBTQ Catholics can continue relating to Jesus regardless of our spiritual journeys. I know that one day, LGBTQ Catholics won't have to leave the Church or hide to protect their well-being. I know that one day, parents of LGBTQ Catholics won't feel like they have to reject their child or "turn them straight" to be good Catholics. I know that one day, parents of LGBTQ Catholics won't have to attend distant parishes to find community. I know that one day the holiness of LGBTQ Catholics who are in a committed relationship will be seen, just like that of those who remain single and abstinent. I know that one day, I won't have to worry about what will happen once God sends into my life that one person whom God has chosen for me, and no, I am not talking about sacramental marriage. I am talking about the simple decency of creating spaces where all of us can continue in relationship with the Church and with God.

I still don't understand why God makes some people like me, but I do know that God made me this way—exactly the way I am. God in his infinite wisdom and in all his mystery has created me, created me with a purpose, a God-given purpose. Perhaps my purpose is to show the world the importance of unconditional love.

For me, being LGBTQ has been a gift, a true blessing. This journey has helped me become a more compassionate, more loving, and more merciful person. It has helped me have a heart of flesh that is not afraid to dig into its own wounds to help others find healing of their own. Mindful of the words of St. Paul, "Now I know only in part; then I will know fully, even as I have been fully known. And now faith, hope, and love abide, these three; and the greatest of these is love" (1 Cor 13:12–13), I know that God is always with me.

I hope that one day your journey of discernment and that of the Church helps us create a community where every part of the Body of Christ is welcome, without fear and prejudice but with love and even, hopefully, celebration!

Appendix A

STORIES OF LGBTQ CATHOLICS

JUSTINE AND DESIREE

As an LGBTQ married couple, we have been fortunate to know each other since high school, and our love and faith have kept us together through ups and downs, sickness and health.

We met in 2000 during our high school years, I was a freshman (in ninth grade) and Desiree was a sophomore (in tenth grade). I first noticed Desiree as I was walking to the softball field to try out and speak with the coaches. I remember being so fascinated by her that I couldn't hear my friends talking. I just remember saying to myself, *I've got to know her name and get to know her.* In that moment, I knew my life would change.

Desiree had no idea that I had noticed her. She remembers me coming to speak to the coaches, but it wasn't until we were both on the team together practicing that I caught her attention. She also seemed fascinated by me. We discovered that we both had mutual friends, so we ended up spending much time together. At first, we were just friends that spent time flirting and being silly with each other. One day, Desiree's cousin told her that I liked her and then gave me her number. We then became inseparable on the phone and wanted to be together whenever possible.

As we got to know each other, neither of us realized that we were both falling in love. Playing on the same team, going to school, and spending time together, it just happened; we fell in love. We officially became girlfriends on July 15, 2000. All was well but there were some obstacles on the journey.

The first challenge was my family. My mom had old-school values and feared me being gay. This scared me; so initially, I decided to keep our relationship private.

Shortly after that, Desiree discovered that she was a few months pregnant from her ex-boyfriend. (Yes, pregnant, in high school, and a lesbian!) That really freaked her out. She broke up with me and tried to do the straight thing with the father. Eventually, she realized that she couldn't force herself to be straight. She learned how to adapt to being a mother and openly gay, but it was a journey.

We knew we couldn't just be friends. Our love was not "friendship" love; it was a deeper, romantic connection. We kept coming back to each other and wanted to be partners for life.

We have been together since 2006 and got married in 2008. We have raised and parented a beautiful young lady who is now a young adult. We have been each other's cheerleader, best friend, and rock. We were fortunate to have had a strong foundation from the very beginning that has seen us through all the highs and lows of our life together.

We found God's love and will not allow anyone to shut out our faith. We continue to go to God and hear and live God's words.

We are currently involved in our local Catholic Church community where we bring an LGBTQ ministry to our Hispanic neighborhood—the first one in our city. We have been blessed to have the support of our pastor and our community.

GREG D. BOURKE AND MICHAEL DE LEON[1]

It was a most unlikely time and place, but on March 20, 1982, Michael and I met at the only gay bar in Lexington, Kentucky. Both in our early twenties and students at the University of Kentucky, we would embark on a relationship that has now spanned nearly forty years. Both cradle Catholics, some of our earliest times spent together were simply practicing our faith at Mass. Despite being an openly gay couple in a hostile social environment and sometimes an unwelcoming Church, we remained devoted to our faith, keeping it at the core of our relationship and lives.

In 1987, we joined Our Lady of Lourdes Catholic Church, less than two blocks from our newly purchased home in Saint Matthews, Kentucky. As openly gay members of the parish, we have been considered novel, if not trailblazers, at the parish. We have been active in many ministries at Lourdes over the decades: parish council, worship committee, boy scout and girl scout leadership, communion ministry, soccer coach, grounds-keeping, resurrection choir, hospitality ministry, stewardship committee, and more.

In 1999, our family expanded with the adoption of our first child, who was followed by a second child adoption in 2000. Our two children were baptized at Lourdes and later attended the parish elementary school. They received their other developmental sacraments at Lourdes, and then attended Catholic high schools in Louisville. Remarkably, our Catholic family was welcomed and treated with great respect and dignity by nearly

---

1. Greg Bourke and Michael de Leon were one of the fourteen same-sex couples and two widowed men who were part of the Supreme Court case Obergefell v. Hodges that led to the legalization of gay marriage in the United States. They are lifelong Catholics.

all they encountered in the Archdiocese of Louisville over the years.

Michael and I were legally married in 2004, in Ontario, Canada, and have been involved in a variety of initiatives to promote LGBTQ equality and inclusion. These efforts went far beyond the Church, as founding members of our respective LGBTQ employee resource groups at GE and Humana. Michael and I were founding members of the University of Kentucky PrideCats Alumni Council, and I was a founding member of the University of Louisville Pride Alumni Council. I have also been a longtime member of GALA-ND/SMC, the LGBTQ alumni group at the University of Notre Dame.

Recently, Michael and I established the first endowed scholarship specifically for LGBTQ Catholic students at the University of Louisville. We also partnered with a small group of parishioners at Lourdes to launch Lourdes Pride, the first LGBTQ ministry sponsored by a parish in the Archdiocese of Louisville. It has been remarkably well received and the ministry has a very bright future at Lourdes and potentially for influencing other ministries throughout the region.

FR. GREGORY GREITEN

Blessings!

I have preached many homilies and written numerous articles. No one really seemed to listen at all. However, a few years ago on the Third Sunday of Advent, I added three words into my homily: "I am gay!" Let me tell you, on that weekend, people took notice and the news of that homily spread quickly. In that homily, I shared that I was choosing to no longer live my life in secrecy, but was embracing a life of honesty, integrity, and authenticity. Later that month, the online edition of the *National Catholic Report* printed my story, "Parish Priest Breaks the Silence, Shares that He Is Gay." The article became the *NCR* edition's breakaway opinion piece for the next year.

I never dreamed that my story was going to touch the lives and hearts of people around the world. Within hours of the story being published, there was an overwhelmingly positive response both nationally and from around the world— Scotland, New Zealand, Australia, Canada, United Kingdom, Argentina, Columbia, Honduras, Mexico, Poland, Germany, Italy, Nigeria, and Uganda. I was deeply touched by the emails, texts, letters, and cards from LBGTQ individuals, as well as their parents, friends, and allies. This article was taken up by other publications and has been translated into German, Polish, Spanish, and Italian.

Some of the responses I received include the following:

A call from a ninety-year-old priest who had no internet connection but read my story in the printed version of the *National Catholic Reporter*. He is also a gay, celibate priest who had lived his entire life in the closet. He called to thank me for writing the article. He was extremely proud that a younger priest was willing to break the silence, speak out, and "come out of the closet." He realized that speaking his truth was simply not an option for him during his ministerial years. He shared that it gave him great hope for the future.

Fr. James Martin, SJ, who is an incredible voice for the LGBTQ community in the Catholic Church wrote, "This man is a pioneer."

A person in New Zealand wrote, "I'm so proud of you for your decision to be open about who God made you to be, and excited by how much this might mean to LGBT Catholics who have felt, and still feel marginalized by their own church. I pray that whatever sexuality my children are gifted by God that their church will welcome and embrace them."

A former student of mine wrote, "I attended St. Mary's School as a young boy when you were our priest and reading about you coming out in the national news today is one of the most comforting things I've read in a long time. A few months ago, I came out, and I was absolutely shocked and humbled when my very Catholic family accepted me and made me feel loved. I can only hope that you have received the same love.... It really gives me hope that you were able to do this; it's a real beacon of light for me. Thank you for your example, not only when I was a child but also today."

Finally, a mom of a seventeen-year-old boy, who came out when he was twelve, wrote, "I told him I was proud of him, loved him, and would always stand by him....My aunt shared her entire adult life with a woman whom she loved dearly and was devoted to until death. She only came out to a handful of people. As a devout Catholic, I think she was torn between who she was and what the Church thought about it....I wish she had lived to read your article."

I can only keep repeating: Be the person that God created you to be! Live your truth. Share your truth with others. Jesus reminds us that "the truth will make you free" (John 8:31–32; ESV).

Appendix B

SAMPLE MISSION/
VISION STATEMENTS

PARISH MINISTRY FOR
LGBTQ CATHOLICS

Agape's Mission

Agape is an inclusive ministry that offers a welcoming and safe environment for all (LGBT+ persons, parents, straight allies, churched, and unchurched people). Through our baptism we are empowered to live a life of discipleship within our Catholic community. The ministry offers pastoral care by listening to people's lived experiences while accompanying each other in our journey of faith. Rooted in the Gospel of Jesus Christ we are called to model God's unconditional love and accept one another as children of God.[1]

---

1. St. John the Baptist Roman Catholic Church, Agape Ministry, "Mission Statement," accessed March 1, 2021, https://www.instagram.com/st.johnsbp.lgbt/?hl=en.

PARISH MINISTRY FOR PARENTS OF LGBTQ CATHOLICS

No Barriers to Christ

Acknowledging that God created us all in His image, each one of us rare and special and wonderfully unique. Then He sent His son to teach us to care for and love one another as we love ourselves. This is a ministry for our Lesbian, Gay, Bisexual, and Transgender brother and sisters, their families, and friends.[2]

Always Our Children

Always Our Children is a support group for parents and loved ones of Lesbian and Gay people, based on the document written by The Bishop's Committee on Marriage and Family. We come together in a safe and confidential environment in which to share our experiences as parents and friends of lesbian and gay children in a Catholic context.[3]

ARCHDIOCESAN MINISTRIES

Archdiocese of Los Angeles Catholic Ministry with Lesbian and Gay Persons (CMLGP)

Believing that baptism empowers all persons to live a full, Catholic life in union with all members of the Church, the Catholic Ministry with Lesbian and Gay Persons provides a safe

---

2. Holy Name of Mary Parish, No Barriers to Christ, "Mission Statement," accessed March 1, 2021, https://www.hnmparish.org/ministry.

3. Archdiocese of Los Angeles, Always Our Children Parent Ministry, accessed March 1, 2021, http://old.la-archdiocese.org/org/cmlgp/Pages/groups.aspx.

and welcoming environment for lesbian and gay persons, their friends and families, through liturgy, outreach, education, and fellowship.

What we do

We speak at schools, parishes, and conferences, educating and dialoguing about inclusivity and acceptance of gays and lesbians within all aspects of Church life. We are an ideal resource for catechists and parents.

We help parishes reach out to their lesbian and gay flock by assistance with organizing and running an outreach ministry. We have resources and experts that will aid your parish in starting a welcoming and inclusive community.

We perform outreach to gay and lesbian events and festivals, providing resources to find welcoming Catholic communities and lend a listening ear to those who feel marginalized by the Church they love.

Our parents' groups provide support and advice for families struggling with acceptance of loved ones who have come out as gay or lesbian.[4]

Diocese of San Bernadino Ministry to Families & Friends with Gay and Lesbian Catholics

Mission Statement

The Bishop's Commission of the Diocese of San Bernadino provides information and resources to the Catholic LGBT community. The Commission supports LGBT Catholics, their families, friends, and parishes as we all walk our journey together

---

4. Archdiocese of Los Angeles, "Catholic Ministry with Lesbian and Gay Persons," accessed March 1, 2021, http://cmlgp.org.

as disciples of Christ. We recognize that all of God's children are gifted and called for a purpose in God's design.

Vision Statement

The Bishop's Commission's main goals are to help everyone:

Understand how to be more inclusive and reach out
to others.
Support LGBT Catholics, their families, and friends.
Educate parish communities to include pastoral care
to LGBT Catholics.
Realize that all are welcome to the table of the Lord.[5]

MINISTRIES BY
RELIGIOUS ORDERS

Marianist Social Justice Collaborative

LGBT Initiative

Working to make the Marianist Family, and the community at large, more welcoming and inclusive of LGBT persons.

Our Mission

The LGBT (Lesbian, Gay, Bisexual, Transgender) Initiative, an issue team of the MSJC, responds to the Church's call to be welcoming and compassionate by offering effective pastoral care and spiritual support for LGBT Catholics and their fami-

---

5. San Francisco Ministry for Gay and Lesbian Catholics, "Mission Statement," accessed March 1, 2021, https://mfglc.wordpress.com.

lies. We foster dialogue, education, and understanding among the diverse communities and institutions affiliated with the Marianist family. Our goal is to fully welcome our Marianist LGBT member into all aspects of our communities. Through our work, we hope the Marianist family becomes a prophetic witness to the Church and the world on how to welcome and embrace LGBT people and their gifts.[6]

HIGHER EDUCATION

Imago Dei

Mission Statement

We are here for those persons who are LGBTQ that are still celebrating their Catholic faith and for those who long to return.

We are also here for families & friends wanting to understand and support their loved one(s) who are LGBTQ.

ALL ARE WELCOME!
WELCOME HOME![7]

---

6. Marianist Social Justice Collaborative, "LGBT Initiative," accessed November 4, 2020, https://msjc.net/lgbt-initiative.

7. Imago Dei, "Mission Statement," accessed November 4, 2020, https:// imagodeilv.wixsite.com/home.

Appendix C
SAMPLE PRAYERS

PARENTS' PRAYER

Thank you, Lord, for each other.
Give us support, understanding and appreciation for
*   where we are in our journey.*
Grant us the serenity to understand the precious
*   ones you have given us and your will for them.*
Turn the darkness around us into light.
Lord, open the hearts and eyes of the parents who
*   have abandoned their children, and bring back*
*   those special children who have left your church.*
Help all our church leaders to show compassion in
*   their ministry.*
All loving God, we place all our thoughts and doubts,
*   biases and viewpoints, plans and confusion into*
*   your hands.*
Lead us in your way.
In your will is peace. Amen.[1]

---

1. Composed by parent members of the Archdioceses of Los Angeles, Catholic Ministry with Lesbian and Gay Persons © 1996. Used with permission.

YOU KNOW MY VOICE

Lord, you are my shepherd,
the one who knows my voice,
recognizes me,
and calls me by name.
You gather me up, hold me close, and feed me.
You strengthen me when I am weak,
heal me when I am sick,
and bind up all my wounds.
Lord, you are my shepherd,
the one who refreshes my soul,
invites me to the table,
and welcomes me to dwell in your House.
I am your homosexual child,
baptized into your flock, O Lord.
My family and I cry out to you for shepherds here on
*   earth—*
in our church and among ourselves—
who, like you, know us, feed us, care for us,
and invite us to your table. Amen.[2]

2. Lynette Aldapa of *Comunidad*, the gay and lesbian ministry of St. Matthew Parish, Long Beach, California, of the Los Angeles Archdiocese Catholic Ministry with Lesbian and Gay Persons © 1996. Used with permission.

BIBLIOGRAPHY

CHURCH DOCUMENTS

Catechism of the Catholic Church. Washington, DC: United States Catholic Conference, 1994.

Congregation for the Doctrine of the Faith. "Letter to the Bishops of the Catholic Church on the Pastoral Care of Homosexual Persons," 1986. http://www.vatican.va.

John Paul II. Apostolic letter *Mulieris Dignitatem*, "On the Dignity and Vocation of Women on the Occasion of the Marian Year." Vatican: Libreria Editrice Vaticana, August 15, 1988. http://www.vatican.va.

John Paul II. "Letter of Pope John Paul II to Women." Vatican: Libreria Editrice Vaticana, 1995. http://www.vatican.va.

National Conference of Catholic Bishops. "Always Our Children." In Vol. 6, *Pastoral Letters of the United States Catholic Bishops*, edited by Patrick W. Carey, 840–50. Washington, DC: United States Catholic Conference, 1998.

———. *To Live in Christ Jesus: A Pastoral Reflection on the Moral Life*. Washington, DC: United States Catholic Conference, 1976.

Pontifical Council for Justice and Peace. *Compendium of the Social Doctrine of the Church*. Vatican: Libreria Editrice Vaticana, 2004. http://www.vatican.va.

Pontificia Commissione Biblica, "'Che Cosa E L'uomo' (Sal 8,5): Un itinerario di antrologia bíblica." Libreria Editrice Vaticana, September 30, 2019. https://www.vatican.va/roman_curia/

congregations/cfaith/pcb_documents/rc_con_cfaith_doc
_20190930_cosa-e-luomo_it.pdf.
United States Catholic Conference. "Human Sexuality: A Catholic Perspective for Education and Lifelong Learning." Washington, DC: United States Catholic Conference, 1991.
———. "Ministry to Persons with a Homosexual Inclination: Guidelines for Pastoral Care." Washington, DC: United States Catholic Conference, 2006.

BOOKS

Bayly, Michael J. *Creating Safe Environments for LGBT Students: A Catholic Schools Perspective*. New York: Routledge, 2012.
Haag, Herbert, Adrianus van den Born, and Serafín de Ausejo. *Diccionario de la Biblia*. Barcelona, Spain: Herder Editorial, 1963.
Helminiak, Daniel. *What the Bible Really Says About Homosexuality*. New Mexico: Alamo Square Press, 2000.
Martin, James. *Building a Bridge: How the Catholic Church and the LGBT Community Can Enter into a Relationship of Respect, Compassion, and Sensitivity*. New York: Harper Collins, 2017.

ARTICLES

DeBernardo, Francis (ed.). "Employees of Catholic Institutions Who Have Been Fired, Forced to Resign, Had Offers Rescinded, or Had Their Jobs Threatened Because of LGBT Issues." New Ways Ministry. Updated June 22, 2020. https://www.newwaysministry.org.

Human Right Campaign. "100 Days Out: Trump v. Biden on LGBTQ Equality in the Workplace." July 23, 2020. https://www.hrc.org.

———. "Sexual Orientation and Gender Identity Definitions." https://www.hrc.org.

Initiative on Public Thought and Life. "Report on National Convening on Lay Leadership for a Wounded Church and Divided Nation." Georgetown University, June 14–15, 2019. https://catholicsocialthought.georgetown.edu.

Maloney, Robert P. "Ten Foundational Principles in the Social Teaching of the Church." *Vincentiana* 43, no. 3 (1999). https://via.library.depaul.edu.

Pickett, Brent. "Homosexuality." In *The Stanford Encyclopedia of Philosophy* (Spring 2021 Edition). Edited by Edward N. Zalta. https://plato.stanford.edu.

Ponnet, Chris, and Arthur Fitzmaurice. "Illuminating Church Teachings on Homosexuality." Religious Education Congress, March 14, 2014. https://lgbtcatholics.files.wordpress.com/2019/03/illuminating-church-teachings-on-homosexuality-recongress2014-handout-3-04.pdf.

Ronan, Wyatt. "New FBI Hate Crimes Report Shows Increases in Anti-LGBTQ Attacks." November 17, 2020. https://www.hrc.org.

Rooney, Caitlin, Charlie Whittington, and Laura E. Durso. "Protecting Basic Living Standards for LGBTQ People." Center for American Progress, August 13, 2018. https://www.americanprogress.org.

Sonoma, Serena. "LGBTQ+ Youth at Increased Risk Of Human Trafficking, New Survey Says." *Out Magazine*, November 2, 2019. https://www.out.com.

Stotzer, Rebecca L. "Data Sources Hinder Our Understanding of Transgender Murders." *American Journal of Public Health* 107, no. 9 (2017): 1362–63. https://www.ncbi.nlm.nih.gov/pmc/articles/PMC5551619/.

Trujillo, Yunuen. "Clerical Sexual Abuse: Religious Institutions Must Have a Pentecost Moment and They Must Have It Now." Berkley Center for Religion, Peace, and World Affairs, Georgetown University, September 25, 2019. https://berkleycenter.georgetown.edu.

Voices of Youth Count. "Missed Opportunities: Youth Homelessness in America." Chapin Hall, University of Chicago, 2017. https://voicesofyouthcount.org.

WEBSITES AND SOCIAL MEDIA

"Always Our Children: A Pastoral Message to Parents of Homosexual Children and Suggestions for Pastoral Ministers." https://www.bishop-accountability.org/resources/resource-files/churchdocs/AlwaysOurChildren.htm.

Archdiocese of Los Angeles: Catholic Ministry for Lesbian and Gay People. http://cmlgp.org.

Courage International. https://couragerc.org.

DignityUSA. https://www.dignityusa.org.

Diocese of San Bernardino: Ministry to Families & Friends with Gay & Lesbian Catholics. https://mfglc.wordpress.com.

Fortunate Families. https://fortunatefamilies.com.

Global Network of Rainbow Catholics. http://rainbowcatholics.org.

Marianist Social Justice Collaborative: LGBT Initiative. https://msjc.net/lgbt-initiative.

New Ways Ministry. https://www.newwaysministry.org.

San Damiano Retreat. https://sandamiano.org.

San Francisco State University: Family Acceptance Project. https://familyproject.sfsu.edu.

St. John the Baptist Roman Catholic Church, Baldwin Park, California: Agape Ministry, Instagram. https://www.instagram.com/st.johnsbp.lgbt/?hl=en.

St. Thomas Aquinas Catholic Newman Center, Las Vegas, Nevada: Imago Dei. https://imagodeilv.wixsite.com/home/connect.

True Colors United, Inc. https://truecolorsunited.org.